A STUDY OF THE LOGIC OF TEACHING

A STUDY OF THE LOGIC OF TEACHING

by B. Othanel Smith and Milton O. Meux

in collaboration with
Jerrold Coombs, Daniel Eierdam, and Ronald Szoke

Published for the College of Education
by the University of Illinois Press
Urbana, Chicago, London

PREFACE

A preliminary report of this study was issued three years ago. The present monograph includes a condensation of the earlier report and a more extended logical analysis of classroom discourse.

The report is divided into three parts. The first part consists largely of materials taken from the preliminary report. Anyone who has read the previous report may skip Part I, turning immediately to Part II which deals with the logical analysis of the episodic materials identified by the procedures described in Part I. Part III attempts to set forth certain problems arising from the entanglement of language, logic, and psychology in the course of instruction.

While this report stands as a unit, it is only fair to note that each chapter was first prepared by a member of the project staff and then read, criticized, and revised by other members of the staff. Chapters II, III, and IV were adapted from the preliminary report. Smith was primarily responsible for Chapters I, VI, and VIII and Meux for Chapters XII and XIV. Chapters X, XI, and XIII were written by Coombs, Chapter IX by Eierdam, and Chapter VII by Szoke.

An investigation of this sort has involved the participation of a large number of individuals. We are of course much indebted to the teachers whose classroom discourse we were permitted to tape, transcribe, and use in this study. We are also grateful to those individuals, too numerous to mention here, with whom discussions were carried on from time to time and from whom a large number of ideas were gained.

CONTENTS

Chapter I

INTRODUCTION

It is generally assumed that effective ways of teaching can
be derived from philosophical and psychological theories. Every theory
of teaching described in the literature is based upon conceptions of
either learning or thinking or both. For example, Kilpatrick's formulation of method is grounded in Dewey's theory of logic and knowledge.
To be sure, he made extensive use of Thorndike's theory of learning,
but this theory is not an essential part of his account of teaching,
as is evidenced by the fact that his later repudiation of Thorndike's
theory necessitated no modification of his theory of teaching.
Furthermore, it is often assumed that if we know how learning occurs,
we thereby know how to teach. For example, it is generally assumed
that if we know how individuals solve problems, then we know how to
teach by the problem method. To teach, in this view, is to see that
the individual does the operations that problem solving requires.

To go from theoretical ideas such as those found in
psychology and philosophy to teaching performance, it is necessary to
work out procedures and materials to bridge the gap between the theory
and the practice. We cannot go directly from theories to practical
applications because there are particular problems that arise with
respect to both materials and procedures. Of course, everyone who
attempts to develop teaching by beginning with philosophy and psychology knows this. But they overlook the fact that to apply any theory
one must understand the phenomenon to which it is to be applied. It
is just as necessary to understand the phenomenon of teaching as a
condition of applying ideas and principles to it as it is to understand the principles and ideas themselves. We must first identify and
describe the dimensions of teaching behavior before we can think
realistically about concepts and principles relevant to its control.

Teaching behavior is made up of a number of interrelated
variables. These variables as well as their relative significance are

for the most part unknown, and those which are assumed to be known are typically conceived in common sense terms. Nevertheless, studies of teaching have been carried on as though the phenomenon of teaching were well understood. For example, there have been investigations of the attitudes of teachers towards their students; studies in permissive and authoritarian behavior of teachers and the effects of such behavior; studies of the intelligence of teachers and their knowledge of subject matter; and inquiries into their personality traits. The failure of such studies to yield a body of consistent knowledge about instruction indicates that perhaps they are premature; that more direct and primitive analyses of teaching behavior are needed as a preface to experimental and correlational studies. Furthermore, such factors as personality traits, intelligence, and knowledge of instructional content are static elements of teaching behavior, indicating nothing about the operations involved in teaching, that is, how concepts, norms, laws, etc., are introduced, analyzed, and manipulated in the course of instruction.

1. Teaching Behavior

As one observes teaching behavior he sees a variety of activities. The teacher asks questions and listens to and appraises answers; listens and responds to students' questions; and reprimands, approves, or reacts neutrally to students. He tells how to do something or shows how it is done. He listens to students tell how to do something or observes their efforts to do it. All of these activities take place in an orderly fashion, and yet they exhibit no readily observable pattern of development. To identify operations within which such elements of teaching behavior have meaning is one of the main tasks of research.

Teaching is assumed here to be a social phenomenon, fundamentally the same from one culture to another and from one time to another in the same culture. It has its own elements, forms, regularities, and problems. It takes place under what seems to be a relatively constant set of conditions -- time limits, authority figures, student ability limits, institutional structures, etc. In its essential features it is a system of social action involving an agent, an end-in-view, a situation and two sets of factors in the situation -- one set over which the agent has no control (e.g., size of classroom and physical characteristics of pupils) and one set which the agent can modify with respect to the end-in-view (e.g., assignments and ways of asking questions). The latter set of factors constitute the means by which ends-in-view are reached. The means, in turn, consists in two types of factors: subject matter and instructional paraphernalia, and the ways of manipulating and maneuvering the subject matter and paraphernalia. The first of these we call material means and the second procedural means. The procedural means have two aspects: large-scale maneuvers which we call strategies, and smaller movements, constituting tactical elements of strategies, which we call logical operations.

'Strategy' refers to a pattern of acts that serve to attain certain outcomes and to guard against certain others. Among the general objectives toward which a strategy may be directed are the following: to insure that certain learnings will be acquired in as brief a time as possible; to induce students to engage in an exchange of ideas; and to minimize the number of wrong responses as the student attempts to learn concepts and principles. We are just beginning a study of strategies, and our conception of them is only in the formative stage.

By 'logical operations', which are the focus of our study, we mean the forms which verbal behavior takes as the teacher shapes the subject matter in the course of instruction. For example, the teacher reduces concepts to linguistic patterns called definitions; he fills in gaps between the student's experience and some new phenomenon by facts and generalizations related in a verbal pattern referred to as explanation; he rates objects, events, etc., by reference to facts and criteria related in a pattern called evaluation. If he does not engage in such operations himself, the teacher either requires his students to do so, or more typically, the teacher and his students jointly carry on these operations through verbal exchanges.

These operations exhibit a structure which can be observed and described. Of course, the structure as it is exhibited in the classroom is often incomplete because the operation is formed elliptically. The teacher may not follow exactly the pattern of a particular type of definition or the complete outlines of a particular form of explanation. Nevertheless, these operations are clearly enough outlined in teaching behavior to be identified and described.

Moreover, these operations can be evaluated logically by reference to rules of validity and correctness, and, while such rules do not describe how a given operation is to be performed, they do afford checking points as to the clarity and rigor of the operation's performance. When teaching behavior takes the form of operations whose patterns can be evaluated by reference to rules of validity and correctness, it is said to be logical.

2. Logic and Psychology in Teaching Behavior

Since this is a study in the logic of teaching perhaps something should be said to distinguish the logic from the psychology of instruction. It is now widely held that teaching can ultimately be explained and controlled by psychological knowledge alone, and that logic is irrelevant to teaching. In the nineteenth century, before psychology became a science and before the rise of the scientific study of pedagogy, no such view of the relation of logic to teaching was held. On the contrary, it was thought that logic described the mental processes involved in both learning and teaching. To DeGarmo and other neo-Herbartians, logicians and philosophers such as Bacon, Mill, and Jevons, and in ancient times, Aristotle, had formulated in their logics the intellectual methods that led to efficient thought and dependable conclusions. It followed, according to their view, that if the teacher mastered the principles of both deductive and inductive logic, he would then be able to employ these methods as he instructs.

This view of the relation between logic and teaching was consistent with the belief of both logicians and psychologists as to the relation between logic and psychology. Logic was supposed to deal

with the laws of the actual processes of thought as well as with the
normative laws of the mind. The laws of logic were the laws of
thought. Pre-scientific psychology, coordinate with this view,
assumed that the laws of logic were implicitly present in the
operations of the mind. Logic and psychology were thus both in agreement as to the role of logic in dealing with mental processes. Hence,
a theory of teaching based upon logic incorporated also what were held
to be sound principles of psychology.

As empirical methods of psychology developed, the notion that
logic dealt with actual mental processes began to be seen as gratuitous.
For one thing, it became evident that ordinary verbal behavior bore
little similarity to the formal logical structures which were the main-
stay of the logicians. For another thing, actual mental processes,
whatever they might be, were unobservable. Hence the question of
whether they were coordinate with logical forms remained at best an
open question.

It is not surprising therefore that the young science of
psychology swept away the whole argument as to the relation of logic
to mental processes. At the very outset, empirical psychology reduced
mental processes to sensations, images, associated mechanisms and the
like. From these psychic elements, it was no longer possible to
construct a set of principles similar to those found in logic. Then,
as experimental animal psychology replaced introspection, consideration
of logical factors of intelligence were again swept aside along with
the whole domain of cognition. In his epic-making studies of animal
intelligence, Thorndike eliminated the possibility of considering
logical elements by reducing thinking and learning to a stimulus-
response model. A response became connected to a stimulus by repeated
temporal association of the two through trial and error, reinforced by
success. Thinking was thus reduced to a series of stimulus-response
actions occurring in accordance with the laws of readiness, exercise,
and effect. And logic, as the science of thinking, was thus completely
undercut.

According to this psychological view, teaching consists in
supplying stimuli and reinforcing correct responses. It also includes

the matching of learning tasks to the drives and motivations of students. This pattern, however, is too simple to be descriptive of teaching behavior as it goes on in the classroom. In the first place, the definition of 'stimulus' is not concise enough to be used in identifying a particular element of the classroom situation as a stimulus. In the second place, instruction is not a simple linear process in which the behavior moves orderly from stimulus to response and on to another stimulus and to another response. Classroom discourse is so branching and so multifarious as to make it almost, if not impossible, to follow a strict chain of stimulus-response behavior.

At the same time that Thorndike and others were advancing experimental psychology, Dewey was reconstructing logic. Working in the context of the Darwinian model -- environmental change, organic variation, selection, and survival -- Dewey formulated the pattern of inquiry which incorporated both inductive and deductive logic as well as psychological facts. Instead of stimulus, he spoke of perplexing situations; instead of learned behavior, Dewey talked of resolved situations brought about by acting in accordance with an appropriate hypothesis. Between the perplexing situation and its resolution, Dewey put reflective thought. Thorndike, on the other hand, filled the gap between stimulus and response with neuron connections. Radical behaviorism excluded even the neurons and thereby eliminated the entire organism as a factor in behavior, reducing psychology to the study of objective conditions under which stimulus and response become associated.

In Dewey's view, logic is grounded in inquiry. The rules of successful inquiry are the rules of logic. And successful inquiry is inquiry which resolves perplexing situations. The rules of inquiry are derived by analyzing what is done as perplexing situations are worked out. When formulated, these rules are the norms by which to assess future inquiries. They may be disengaged from inquiry and studied in and of themselves, as in formal logic. Thus formalized, they are apt to lose their connection with inquiry, and in consequence, their normative role in reflective behavior.

From Dewey's theory of logic, educational psychologists derived the theory of problem-solving, and Kilpatrick his project method of teaching. Both Kilpatrick and the psychologists ignored the normative aspects of Dewey's logical theory and emphasized his psychological elements. The theory of motivation, as well as the theory of learning which came to play a dominant role in educational thought, centered in this psychologized version of Dewey's theory of logic. Its central idea is that the individual is moved to act when he is in an unsettled situation -- one for which he has ready-made response. In such a situation, the individual is moved to try various ways of acting to overcome the barrier to his reaching a goal. By working himself out of such circumstances, he learns. Teaching, according to this view, consists in guiding the learner through the process of discovery and verification. Today, there is an emphasis upon teaching by the problem method, by the method of discovery, and the like. In this version of inquiry and teaching, there is no distinction between valid and invalid thinking, for such distinction cannot be made within this kind of psychological analysis of problem-solving.

There are indications today that perhaps this separation of logic and psychology has been overemphasized. Piaget has shown that even the non-verbal behavior of the child involves the performance of certain logical operations. When these operations are looked at from the standpoint of what an individual does when he performs them, they are descriptions of behavior and as such are psychological in character. On the other hand, when these operations are analyzed from the standpoint of how well they conform to ideal models, they are being construed from a logical standpoint. Working in a somewhat different frame of reference, Bruner in his analysis of thinking has shown that an individual may follow any one of a number of strategies in the attainment of a concept. These strategies are descriptive of the behavior which an individual exhibits as he attempts to achieve a concept which is implicitly present in the behavioral situation. Viewed from a logical standpoint, these strategies are similar to Mill's so-called methods of induction. It thus appears that how behavior is to be considered depends upon the standpoint from which it is observed. When it is observed as a process, it is held to be psychological. When it is observed in terms of how well it measures up to certain rules of validity and correctness, it is thought to be logical.

We thus see that there is a tendency in current psychology to investigate and describe the operations which logicians are concerned to evaluate in terms of the rules of logic. The study of teaching herein reported falls in this new tendency to focus both psychology and logic upon similar forms of behavior. It could be said that when we are looking at the performance of the operation we are studying teaching behavior from a psychological standpoint. When we are examining the operation from the standpoint of its structure and the rules by which it is evaluated, we are looking at teaching behavior logically.

3. Outlines of Procedure

The study reported herein is neither an evaluative nor an experimental investigation of teaching. No attempt is made to determine the effects of teaching behavior upon students. Nor is there an attempt to establish correlations among variables or to search for causes of teacher behavior. Rather, this study is an analytic and descriptive one in the natural history sense. An effort is made to develop a way of dividing verbal teaching behavior into pedagogically significant units, and to analyze the units in logically meaningful ways.

Since descriptive research is sometimes depreciated, perhaps something should be said in its defense. If very little is known about a phenomenon, the way to begin an investigation of it is to observe and analyze the phenomenon itself. It must be observed, analyzed, and classified into its various elements. Until the factors which are involved in the phenomenon are understood and described, there is little likelihood that significant correlational, predictive, or causal studies can be made. In other words, the state of knowledge about a given phenomenon dictates to some extent the kind of study of it which is appropriate. A justification therefore of a descriptive study of teaching is that it is preliminary to experimental investigation of the phenomenon itself.

A descriptive study can be focused at different levels of

analysis. The choice of level is dependent upon the purpose. For example, it is possible to analyze steel in different ways and at different levels. One can determine the amount of stress steel will bear; the pliability of the metal and its ability to recover its position if a column of it is displaced under stress; and its tendency to disintegrate under intense vibration. It can be analyzed into its components -- the percentage of carbon it contains or the amount of any other metal with which it is alloyed. Its atomic structure can be determined. What one chooses to describe about steel will depend upon his purpose. If one is building a bridge, it is obvious that some of these analyses will be irrelevant. The engineer may be interested in the stress-bearing qualities of the steel or in its tolerance for vibration, but he may have no interest, or at least only incidental interest, in the structure of its atoms.

So it is with teaching behavior. It is possible to analyze teaching behavior into very minute elements. After the fashion of behavioristic psychology, an investigator may attempt to identify the stimulus factor in teaching behavior; the response factor; reinforcement factor; and so on. Or he may attempt to identify larger units of teaching behavior after the fashion of Piaget's studies of the behavior of children. For example, he may attempt to find out whether or not teaching behavior involves operations of logical order such as symmetry, asymmetry, and transitivity. Or he may attempt to identify still larger units of behavior. In the current study, a deliberate choice was made with respect to the level of analysis. It is concerned with molar aspects of teaching behavior -- logical performances verbally executed.

Since verbal behavior perishes as it occurs and is too complex to be observed and analyzed immediately, it is necessary to record it. Only when it is recorded and can thus be repeatedly observed, can it be used as a source of data for the analysis of teaching. For these reasons, it was decided to base this study upon data derived from tape recordings of classroom discussion. The discourse thus recorded occurred at the high school level in the conventional content fields --

sciences, English, social studies, and mathematics.

Once recordings were made, transcribed, and reproduced in dittoed form, the task was to work out some suitable way of describing the discourse. One way to describe discourse is to analyze it into units. Of course, there are many different units of discourse -- words, sentences, paragraphs, etc. But the purpose of this investigation made it necessary that the unit be related significantly to instruction. One of the units finally worked out is a unit of discourse beginning with an expression which triggers a verbal exchange about a topic and ending with a completion of the discussion of that topic. This unit we call an episode. The other unit of discourse, in which there is one and only one speaker, we refer to as a monolog.

The next step consisted in working out logical categories into which episodes could be sorted. After the episodic units were classified into logical categories, the episodes of each category were analyzed to ascertain their logical structures. Where it was possible to contrive a model of the logical structure, this model has been presented. We then classified the episodes of a given category into subcategories in accordance with certain criteria. Then by presenting actual episodes of each subclass we attempted to show how the episodic material conforms to and departs from the model. In other words, the analysis which we have made of each episode is broadly speaking logical, rather than psychological or linguistic.

The question naturally arises as to whether or not the quality of teaching behavior is in some way related to the performance of these logical operations. A number of questions come to mind: Is learning concise modes of thought related to the degree in which teaching behavior conforms to the complete structure of each of these operations? Or, is it related to the degree in which the student is required to bring his own verbal behavior into line with the strict pattern of these operations? Or, is the student better able to monitor his own thinking as well as that of others if he has knowledge of the logical structure and rules governing the performance of these operations? Does an explicit understanding of these operations increase the student's knowledge of the subject he is studying? Does the more rigorous performance of these operations require that the teacher have command of his subject matter in ways different from that which he ordinarily possesses? Would the ability of a teacher to explore subject matter logically free him from overdependence upon the textbook? Should answers to these questions be affirmative, would not knowledge about these logical operations and how to perform them constitute a new content for courses in pedagogy? Such questions as these go beyond the purpose and design of the present investigation. They are in general experimental in import, and can hardly be answered apart from a more thorough understanding of these logical operations in their pedagogical context, especially the way in which they are related sequentially to particular objectives and in the sorts of strategies in which they are imbedded.

PART ONE

Chapter II

THE UNITS OF CLASSROOM DISCOURSE

To analyze the mass and variety of verbal behavior recorded
in the transcripts, two kinds of units were developed: episode and
monolog. The episode is a multispeaker unit; it consists in the one
or more exchanges which comprise a completed verbal transaction
between two or more speakers. The monolog, a single-speaker unit, is
the solo performance of an individual addressing the classroom group.

1. Requirements for a Unit

The unit of classroom discourse must be more than a means
merely of chopping up a mass of words -- say a twenty-page transcript
of a forty-minute class session -- into small bits. Such a unit must
satisfy a number of requirements: it must be logically analyzable,
neutral with respect to content, and reliable. These requirements may
be stated more fully as follows.

First, the unit must facilitate an examination of those
aspects of verbal behavior which it would be most relevant to an
analysis of the logical dimensions of teaching.

Second, the unit must be neutral. By a neutral unit is
meant one that would take on the same form regardless of its content.
A unit in a geometry class transcript should resemble a unit in an
English transcript. Such a unit is capable of examination from any
number of standpoints, and is classifiable, as a unit, into a variety
of categories. Upon this basis, qualitative, comparative, and
quantitative analyses can be made.

A final requirement is that of reliability. The unit must
be one which, ideally, would permit any trained analyst to identify
the same units in a given set of transcripts that any other analyst,
equally trained, would find independently in the same set.

2. The Unit of Discourse

An episode, it will be recalled, is defined as the one or more exchanges which comprise a completed verbal transaction between two or more speakers. The monolog, on the other hand, consists in the solo performance of a speaker addressing the group. Division of the discourse into these two kinds of units exhausts the discourse. Where one unit ends the next begins. We shall now set forth in some detail these two basic forms.

Episodic discourse. In its normal course, a discussion in progress exhibits a characteristic development. Certain forms of utterances are used to enjoin or invite immediate reply; other forms are conventionally understood to forestall or prohibit immediate response. A direct question, addressed either to a given person or to the group at large, conventionally demands some kind of responding action on the part of the individual or group addressed. A rhetorical question, on the other hand, is commonly understood to be uttered for its dramatic or rhetorical effect, but some do serve to trigger discussion. When a reply is made to a direct question, it is also a convention that the reply itself be acknowledged in some way, at least by word or gesture if not by further responding commentary or questioning. These and other forms of verbal behavior fall together into definite patterns in the course of a discussion.

We have encountered two patterns of episodic discourse. In each of the patterns there is a remark which serves to launch the verbal transaction. We call the remarks which act in this way entries. In the first pattern, called the reciprocating pattern, alternation between two speakers occurs after the entry -- back and forth movement so aptly described as reciprocating action. In the other pattern, called the coordinate pattern, each successive speaker responds more or less directly to the entry rather than to the remarks of the immediately preceding speaker. Hence each utterance following the entry is coordinate with all the others, with respect to that entry and to the utterance closing the episode.

The following series of three episodes[1] illustrates the <u>reciprocating</u> pattern.[2]

*

Episode 1   *T: <u>Now who do you know who was the first person who discovered the Hawaiian Islands?</u> Steve?

Steve: Was it Captain Cook?

T: That's right. // <u>Do you know about what time it was</u>, Steve?

Steve: 1670 something?

T: No, it's not that early. Come down about a hundred years.

Steve: 1770?

T: Yes. It was 1778, actually during the time of our American Revolution. // <u>And do you know what he called the islands?</u> They weren't Hawaii at the time. Anybody know? Oh, I think this is an easy name to remember -- especially around noon. Steve?

Steve: Cook Islands?

T: No. They weren't Cook Islands. That's a good guess, but that doesn't happen to be it. The Sandwich Islands.

Steve: Oh.

T: Do you eat sandwiches at noon, too? // In this particular period, the United States wasn't too interested. Of course, we were concerned with gaining our freedom from England at that particular time, but soon after that... etc.

*

In her second utterance, the teacher confirms Steve's reply to her original question and then proceeds to ask him a new question. Her confirming 'That's right' closes the first episode; her new question is the entry which opens the second episode. This series of reciprocating episodes closes with the teacher's play on words, after which she launches into a monolog.

---

[1] From a U. S. History class, grade 11.

[2] In this excerpt, a broken line underscores the entry in each episode. Paired diagonal lines have been placed as indicators for the breaking points between episodes.

* 'Teacher' is abbreviated as 'T' throughout the report.

It should be noted that the same two speakers carried on the three transactions. Episodes are determined not by shifts in speakers, but by shifts in what the speakers are talking about, and by the speech forms and patterns of their dealings with the point under discussion. In the first episode the point of concern is the identity of the discoverer of the Hawaiian Islands. The second episode focuses upon a different point: the date of the discovery. When this question is settled, the teacher and Steve move on, in the third episode, to the point concerning the name first given the Hawaiian Islands. In each case their dealings with the current point goes through a three-phase pattern: the point is raised in an entry (opening phase); a reply is ventured, judged, or the like (continuing phase); the exchanges are then either sustained further or dropped by the teacher's conventional acknowledging (closing) remark. Reciprocating episodes vary in many ways from the simple paradigm illustrated in the first of the three episodes above. Nevertheless, each reciprocating episode stands as a discrete unit, as a completed verbal transaction.

Below is a typical example of an episode corresponding to the coordinate pattern. The point under discussion concerns the question of a novelist's use of his story as a medium for propaganda:[3]

*

Episode 2 T: All right, now, as Carol pointed out, Alan Paton is pleading for the alternative solution -- that of brotherly love or peaceful co-existence between the races. Now, what do you think of a novelist who tries to preach a lesson or to promote his point of view through the medium of fiction? You think of that. Mary?

 Mary: I was just going to say that I think it's the type of the novel. I mean it's the way that it is presented that moves us. He could present it in different ways if he wanted to. Not necessarily the -- the novel or -- oh, something that teaches you a moral lesson.

 T: All right, just as we discussed, it's a short story. Some stories do have a moral lesson to preach and then they become parables rather than just generalized short stories. And others

---

[3] From an English class, grade 11.

simply are entertaining. Denny?

Denny: Well, I think that more people would be interested
        in the fiction form of the novel than in just a
        pamphlet giving specific reasons why the two races
        should live together in brotherhood. I think it
        would attract more attention and be more interesting.

Judy: Well, since it's -- When people read it, it's
       more parallel to everyday life. You might be
       able to understand it a lot better in a novel and
       so on. Otherwise, you just see these facts and
       you wouldn't associate yourself and how you would
       feel and react to it.

T: All right. // Well, now, the chief function of
    any kind of fiction is to entertain, isn't it?
    Do you feel that in this book, Cry the Beloved
    Country, the author is actually entertaining you?

*

The entry which triggers this episode is the teacher's
question: 'Now, what do you think of a novelist....fiction?' Mary
responds and the teacher acknowledges, 'All right,', adding a
supplementary comment. Then Denny and Judy each respond to the point,
one after the other. The teacher acknowledges their remarks without
comment, then uses a rhetorical device to preface the next entry: her
question about whether Alan Paton's novel entertains its readers.

Note the characteristic structure of the coordinate episode:
each student responds to the entry rather than to what his classmates
have said, so that the effect is that of a series of utterances
related only by the fact that they are all addressed to the same point.
In this type of episode there is no direct verbal exchange between
teacher and student or student and student as is found in the
reciprocating pattern.

It should be pointed out that these two episodic patterns
are sometimes mixed. That is, both the coordinate and reciprocating
patterns of verbal interplay occur within the same episode. Below is
an example of a mixed-pattern episode.[4] The discussion is concerned

---

[4] From an English class, grade 11.

with some of the central characters in Alan Paton's <u>Cry, the Beloved Country</u>. The teacher is referring to one of them, John Kumalo, an ardent proponent of black supremacy in Africa, as she begins the episode.

*

Episode 3   T: <u>What is his particular talent that is being used in this organization</u>? Mary?

   Mary: His lion's voice?

     T: His lion's voice? Was that it?

   Mary: Well, he had a real booming voice.

     T: Bill?

   Bill: He had his -- I was thinking about when they -- you know -- get them all shook up or something like that and then they -- [A boy breaks in: "Oh! I'm all shook up!" laughter from class.] You know what I mean, well -- you know like -- well, I don't know how you explain to a --

     T: I know what you mean, but I can't say it.

  Lydia: He had the power to agitate -- to get people -- to kind of -- he appealed mostly to their emotions and he'd get them so far, then he'd just sort of -- just some way -- decide to -- that they're hungry and some people would say -- for food and he -- more and more and he got -- putting into propositions the -- natural way -- keep them from doing it.

     T: At one point, isn't his voice called "old Grundage" -- isn't that one of the descriptions that Paton uses? And his particular talent of leadership of the group that he's working with is to be an impassioned speaker -- you can just picture him on a street corner getting everybody all riled up. // <u>Who else belonged to this leadership on the side that -- if it were to win, were to lead to black supremacy</u>?

*

This mixed episode moves through several reciprocating exchanges between Mary and the teacher. Then Bill and Lydia join in, each responding to the entry rather than to what Mary said. Hence Bill's and Judy's remarks coordinate with Mary's with respect to the entry. The teacher closes the discussion with some elaborative comments and then launches a new episode with the entry 'Who else belonged....etc.?'

It should be noted, incidentally, that episodes are not always brought through a final or closing phase, as are those presented here to illustrate typical episodic forms. Quite often one episode will be terminated without any explicit closing comment or assent; instead, the transaction is closed tacitly by the advent of a new entry, that is, of an utterance advancing some new point, which, in turn, triggers more response. There is nothing out of the ordinary about a discussion which proceeds through such a series of truncated episodes. They are merely common phenomena of group verbal activity.

Monolog discourse. The second form in which units of classroom discourse may be identified embodies the alternate basic element of group verbal behavior: the "solo performance" of a speaker addressing the group. For an example of how monolog discourse typically occurs during class sessions, let us return to the U. S. History class that we observed in a discussion of the Hawaiian Islands. The teacher has been talking with Steve, it will be recalled. She turns from their play on words and launches into the following monolog:

*

Monolog 1   T: Do you eat sandwiches at noon, too? // In
                 this particular period, the United States
                 wasn't too interested. Of course, we were
                 concerned with gaining our freedom from England
                 at that particular time, but soon after that we
                 began to send people out around the world to
                 trade and, of course, to stop at one of -- many
                 of them would stop at the Hawaiian Islands. The
                 first people who went out there to settle, how-
                 ever, were not traders. Do you know what their
                 interest was? Do you remember what their interest
                 was? They went in 1820, the very first Americans
                 in the islands -- who settled in the islands.
                 They were missionaries, and they were going out
                 to try and christianize the heathens. Then
                 people who were interested in trade and farming
                 in particular went into the islands and their
                 concern, of course, was the raising of sugar
                 cane.
                     And that brings us down into the period of
                 history that we have been discussing more recently--

when they were trying to make treaties which
would make it possible for them to trade with
the United States -- particularly to get rid
of their sugar in the United States. And the
first trade treaty was made in the 1870's. It
was a reciprocal trade treaty in which one
particular product from Hawaii was to be admitted
to the United States free. The product was, of
course, the one which they had in greatest
quantity at that time -- sugar. In 1880, they
renewed that treaty, and the United States got
the right to use a particular coaling base --
coaling station there. // Now, do you have any
idea which base we acquired in the 1880's --
the use of which base? One that you should
recognize. A very prominent part in the American
defense system today. Tony?

Tony: Pearl Harbor?

T: Pearl Harbor. That's right. And we have had a
base there at Pearl Harbor, then, since 1880. //
Now, how did the United States first become aware
of the problem of ...? etc.

*

The excerpt above stands as almost a model of a teacher's
monolog. It is also quite typical of the way in which many teachers
move from discussion to lecture and back to discussion again.

Monolog discourse does not reveal phase-like qualities, as
in episodic interplay. However, expository monologs in progress exhibit
a kind of paragraph-to-paragraph movement. This is seen in the teacher's
monolog above -- indicated by an indentation -- as she shifts from the
topic of early settlers of the Hawaiian Islands to that of the trade
treaties between the Hawaiian Islands and the United States. A solo
speaker often moves from point to point in his exposition, raising it,
elaborating at some length, and then proceeding to some further point.

Monologs are usually found in the didactic or expository
discourse of the teacher. However, in his role as leader and arbiter
of class proceedings, the teacher also delivers in monolog form, upon
occasion, announcements, assignments, and sometimes admonishments and
moral preachments. Student monologs generally consist in such verbal
activity as the presentation of assigned reports.

Monologs occur much less frequently than do episodes, although there is variation from class to class. This is to be expected, since monolog performances are quite normally reserved for special purposes and special occasions in group discussion proceedings.

Although no analysis of monologs has been made for this report, it probably would be useful in further analyses of classroom discourse to take note of these paragraph-like passages in a didactic monolog for the relation their contents may have to prior and subsequent class discussion.

3. Criteria for Identifying Units

Episodes and monologs are identified by means of criteria. Before giving the criteria we shall set forth certain definitions which are useful in understanding the criteria and in applying them in the analysis of classroom discourse.

A. Discourse: All of the verbal behavior occurring during a class period.

B. Utterance: The complete record of the verbal behavior of one individual at one point or another within an episode. Exclamations such as "m-m" by the teacher, where concurrent with the student's verbal behavior, do not count as utterances.

C. Episode: A unit of discourse involving a verbal exchange between at least two individuals. It passes typically through three phases: (a) an initial or opening phase, (b) a sustained or continuing phase, and (c) a terminal or closing phase.

    c:1 The initial or opening phase of an episode always contains a remark or set of remarks (assertions, questions, announcements, etc.) which is called an entry.

        c:11 Remarks of other types may occur within the opening phase. These may function as introductory or prefatory to the entry.

    c:2 The continuing phase of an episode contains remarks launched directly by the entry, or indirectly by one or more remarks which were directly launched by the entry.

    c:3 The terminal or closing phase of an episode may contain remarks designed either to supplement preceding remarks or to cut off the flow of discussion. In the absence of closing remarks, the terminus of an episode is marked only by the advent of verbal moves characteristic of the opening phase of a new episode.

D. A monolog is an extended unit of discourse spoken by an individual and which does not exhibit episodic form. In addition, the monolog differs from episodes in that no other speaker is involved in any sort of verbal exchange, except by intrusion or interruption.

Criteria. The criteria used in identifying episodes and monologs are as follows:

1. An entry consists of a remark or set of remarks (question, assertions, etc.) signalizing that it will be followed by discussion, and setting the direction of that discussion.

   1.1 The entry launches or advances the discussion in a new direction. An advance of discussion in a new direction is marked by:

      1.11 A complete change in the topic or subject of discussion.

      1.12 The introduction of a new aspect or part of a topic, subject, or argument of which one part was treated in a prior episode. This new aspect may have been mentioned in the initial or opening phase of a prior episode, but not be specifically taken up or developed in that episode.

         1.121 Calling for further instances or cases of the topic or subject under discussion, except for simple enumeration of instances, shall count as an entry.

      1.13 Returning to a point discussed in a prior episode and subsequently dropped, but to which the speaker now enlists or enjoins further discussion, shall count as an entry.

   1.2 If a speaker advances a claim or raises a question or issue not being considered, and if he does so by invitation, consent, or simply on his own rather than on demand, his remark shall count as an entry.

   1.3 If an entry statement is repeated after one or more episodes have intervened since the entry was first introduced, it shall count as an entry if it satisfies all other requirements for an entry.

   1.4 A remark or set of remarks is said to be an abortive entry if it fails to elicit response even though it may satisfy all other entry requirements.

   1.5 An entry does not engage the preceding speaker in clarifying or continuing what he just said. But it may be addressed to the preceding speaker, either directly or by implication.

   1.6 An entry is not a statement that has been required, enjoined, or sought for by the preceding speaker.

2. The continuing phase of an episode is made up of remarks which are:

(a) either replies or responses to questions; (b) claims, comments, or opinions; (c) questions which sustain the entry or point under discussion; and (d) anomalous questions.

2.1 A reply is a verbal move (remark) made in answer to a question that was addressed to the individual giving the answer.

2.2 A response is a verbal move (remark) made in answer to a question that was addressed at large rather than to a particular individual.

2.3 Claims, comments, or opinions addressed to the point under discussion in the episode are neither replies nor responses. They serve to sustain the flow of discussion.

2.4 Questions serve to sustain the continuing phase of an episode if they either direct attention to a prior question, or if they take up the point of a prior remark.

    2.41 Questions which direct attention back to a prior question in the episode:

        2.411 Replication: These questions repeat the entry question, or any other question, in the same words. They usually occur when the first rendering of a question was not heard or attended to.

        2.412 Rephrasing: These questions repeat the point of the entry question, or of any other question, but in somewhat different words. These questions usually occur when a question was not understood or when the answer to the original question was unsatisfactory.

        2.413 Reshaping: These questions go beyond rephrasing in that the content of the original question is somewhat altered. This alteration returns attention to the intent (purport) of the original question by pointing out an emphasis implied in the original formulation but which apparently needed explicit rendering.

    2.42 Questions which develop or elaborate the point of a prior question or statement by:

        2.421 Asking for amplification, clarification, information, evidence, or justification of what a speaker has said.

        2.422 Asking or calling for personal opinion, preferences, or judgments directly concerning the point being considered. Such requests may be addressed either to an individual or to the group at large.

    2.43 Anomalous questions:

2.431 Rhetorical: These are assertions in question form. They are usually made to invite agreement, to give information, or to elicit supplementary comments.

2.432 Designative: These are questions which have nothing do do with the content of discussion but rather with the designation of who should or may speak. An individual may be designated, or the question may be addressed at large.

2.433 Come-back signal: This is a question or a statement which has nothing to do with the content of discussion. It is used as a signal to the preceding speaker that his last remark was unintelligible, inaudible, or otherwise in need of restatement.

2.434 Review: These are questions which are asked to refresh one's memory about what was said earlier in the episode or even in a preceding episode.

3. An episode may pass through an overtly terminal phase or be closed off by the abrupt change of topic or subject which signals the opening of a new episode.

3.1 The overtly closing phase of an episode includes remarks which serve expressly to cut off the flow of discussion. This cutting off may be effected by the repetition of the last statement of the continuing phase, or by such expressions as "All right," "O.K.," etc.

3.2 The close of an episode is often marked by the occurrence of supplementary or elaborate comments which serve to punctuate the current flow of discussion.

3.3 In the absence of remarks expressly cutting off discussion or of supplementary comment, the episode is taken as terminated by the occurrence of remarks which signal the opening of a new episode.

4. A monolog, as a feature of classroom discourse, stands as a unit.

4.1 It is marked by the introduction of one or more new topics or subjects, or of one or more new aspects of a topic or subject previously mentioned or discussed.

4.2 The treatment of the materials introduced in monolog discourse is carried on entirely by a single speaker, and sustained by him without verbal exchange with other speakers, except in the event of intrusions or interruptions.

4.3 As a unit of discourse, a monolog satisfies neither the criteria of being supplementary in the closing phase of an episode, nor of being prefatory in the opening phase; nor can it be counted as a feature of the continuing phase of an episode.

The instrument reproduced above would be useless to anyone lacking the conceptual and technical background which it presupposes on the part of the analyst. It was designed for use by a group of analysts who were already familiar with our conception of verbal behavior and already experienced in the study of classroom transcripts. By the time we arrived at the present set of criteria a common conceptual and procedural frame of reference had been attained for those who took part in its development.

Some features of the instrument should be noted. It presents four groups of criteria. Each group is numbered, and each criterion has its own number within a group. All criteria of the number 1 group concern the identification of entry moves in episodes. Criteria in groups 2 and 3 cover the kind of remarks found in sustaining and terminating phases of episodes, respectively. The fourth group of criteria is used to identify monologs.

The procedure for marking off a transcript is as follows. The analyst tags each utterance with one or more numbers from the set of criteria: more than one if the utterance contains, e.g., both continuing and closing phases, both closing and opening phases, etc. Each number represents his judgment concerning the identity of the particular remark or remarks made in the utterance. With utterances which start or contain the start of an episode, the procedure is somewhat more complicated: (1) If the beginning of the utterance also is the beginning of the episode, the analyst draws a line between the previous utterance and the utterance starting a new episode. (2) If the beginning of the utterance is not the beginning of the episode, but the new episode starts within the utterance (e.g., with the second or third sentence), then the analyst draws a line within the utterance separating the close of the previous episode from the start of the new episode.

We made it a matter of standard procedure, in the early applications of the instrument, always to affix the criterion numbers to each utterance. This practice not only facilitated testing, since disagreements in judgment were thus quickly located; it also provided each analyst with a means of checking self-consistency in his judgments. This practice of tagging each utterance is dropped as the analyst gains sufficient experience with the criteria. Then he only marks episode boundaries as described in the previous paragraph.

We do not consider the present form of the instrument final. Its formulation is still relatively crude at certain points, and could readily be refined and more succinctly worded. It is also likely that additions and revisions may be made in the continued application of the criteria to transcribed discussions. However, it is not likely that any set of criteria could be developed which would account for any and every item of verbal behavior that may occur in discussion. For language is as infinitely varied in its forms as the human activity of which it is a part.

Reliability of the Criteria. The type of reliability estimate used to assess the dependability of these criteria was a coefficient of inter-judge agreement, one based on percentage of agreement between independent judgments. The experimental phase of the determiniation of reliability involved obtaining independent judgments of the episodic breaking points of the transcripts. The formula for calculating the coefficient was a simple one involving the percentage of agreements out of the total number of units marked.

Four staff members of the project were used to obtain the independent judgments required for the reliability test. These staff members had not participated in the development of the criteria. We felt it to be important that a training procedure be followed with the judges to acquaint them with the type of data being dealt with and especially to clarify the conceptual framework within which their judgments were to be made.

The material used to train the judges consisted in actual transcripts of class sessions. Two of the transcripts -- one English and one Social Studies -- were chosen on which to base the training. These were selected to provide some variation in subject matter while at the same time not overwhelming the new judges (novel material, task, etc.).

The training procedure for the judges involved studying the criteria, marking the training transcripts individually, and discussing difficulties with the staff members who had developed the criteria.

The material used for the actual reliability estimates consisted of seven transcripts: three in eleventh-grade U. S. History and four in eleventh-grade English.

The first step of the final testing consisted in each of the four judges marking off independently what he judged to be the total set of units (both episodes and monologs) on each transcript. He numbered each utterance with the number of the criterion he thought it satisfied. The judges were instructed to distinguish the greatest number of units which could result from applying the criteria.

In the second step of the final testing, the four judges worked in two teams of two judges each. Within each team, the two judges together considered each utterance in the light of the criteria and their original assessments of each utterance. After this step, many disagreements were eliminated; others persisted.

These combined results from each pair were used for the coefficients of agreement.[5] The formula for the coefficient is:

$$R = \frac{A_{xy}}{\text{Max}\ (E_x,\ E_y)}$$

where A_{xy} is the number of agreements between teams X and Y, E_x is the total number of episodes marked by team X, E_y is the total number of episodes marked by team Y, and Max (E_x, E_y) is the maximum value of the two teams E_x and E_y (i.e., the numerically larger of the two numbers, E_x and E_y.) The coefficients obtained are presented in Table 1.

---

[5] We felt that it was better to use the combined judgment of a pair of judges because of the complexity of both the material in the transcripts and the criteria themselves. These factors tend to result in a number of "sheer oversights" and accidental skips in using the criteria, and can be reduced significantly by using pairs of judges to arrive at the units.

Table 1. Coefficients of agreement for the criteria,
based on selected tapes from U. S. History
and English

Tape Number and Subject	Coefficient
1 U.S. History	.71
2 U.S. History	.73
3 U.S. History	.62
4 English	.71
5 English	.70
6 English	.64
7 English	.69

The coefficients range from .62 to .73 -- a fairly small range -- with a median of .70.

Disagreements seem to stem mostly from vagueness or ambiguity of utterances. Because of the many subtle shadings and nuances in behavior, utterances are often not clearly specifiable as fitting one criterion or another. One particular discrimination we have consistently had trouble with is in applying criteria where the judge must distinguish between a new aspect of the same topic and a clarification or amplification of some point in the topic. We have been unable as yet to formulate a general and consistent rule to eliminate these difficulties. Another difficulty arises in distinguishing between long prefatory material and monologs.

Chapter III

CLASSIFICATION OF EPISODES

Episodes can be classified in a number of ways: by the nature of their content, by the number of verbal interactions they involve, by the psychological processes they entail, and so on. In this study episodes are to be classified in terms of their logical features. To classify episodes in this way it is first necessary either to invent categories or to use those found already in the domain of logic, and second, to work out criteria for deciding whether a given episode belongs to a particular category. We shall treat the development of categories and their criteria in this chapter.

1. Entries as the Basis of Classification

As we began the task of working out a classificatory scheme for episodes, the question arose as to whether the entire episode or only a particular part of it was to be considered. We could classify the opening phases and thereby group episodes by these phases. Or we could use either the continuing or the closing phase as the basis of classification. Or again, we could classify the episodes without regard to their parts.

Certain considerations led us to classify episodes by their opening phases. The opening phase always contains a verbal move which evokes at least one, but more often a series of related verbal exchanges. We have called this verbal move an entry. It is always a self-initiating move on the part of the person who makes it and it is followed by responding remarks. The entry thus tends to shape the character of the episode. If the entry calls for the meaning of a word, the continuing phase is apt to consist of statements telling how the word in question is used. Likewise if the entry calls for an explanation, the continuing phase will likely emphasize statements which give reasons for or otherwise account for an action, event, etc. Of course, it is not necessarily the case that the continuing phase will be consistent with the demands of the entry. The student may misunderstand the entry. He may not know how to respond and thereby fumble the verbal exchange. Or for some other reason the student may fail to make an appropriate response. In any event, there is not always a close logical correspondence between what the entry calls for and what the body of the episode contains. For this reason, we chose to use the entry as the cue to the purport of the episode rather than the continuing phase of the unit.

2. The Development of Categories

At the outset it seemed possible to select ready-made categories from among those found in works on logic. If such selection were possible, the remaining task would consist of devising criteria and procedures for placing episodes in appropriate categories. However, it soon became clear that no such simple solution was possible. The great variety and complexity of symbolic operations demanded by teachers made it quite clear that episodes could not be neatly fitted into ready-made classes. It was necessary to follow a more empirical procedure -- to work out categories in terms of the nature of the entries themselves. Of course, conventional categories of logic such as definition, designation, and classification appear in our list of categories. This is necessarily the case. To refuse to use such categories would be to invent a new logic, and that task is not within our domain. But the occurrence of these categories in our list resulted from study of the entries themselves rather than from a priori decisions.

One effort to formulate categories empirically was focused upon an analysis of the verbs contained in the entries. It seemed likely that the nature of the main verb would be a clue to the logical demands of the entry. The entry 'What is the bigger part of the brain called?' contains the verbal expression 'is ----- called'. Entries containing such expressions would seem to fall into a logical category of term-referent where the referent is given and the name of it is called for. Again, the expression 'do ---- differ' appearing in the entry 'How do the eyes of the fish differ from the eyes of the invertebrates that we have been talking about?' seems to indicate clearly that this entry requires some sort of discrimination, a pointing out of the differences between the eyes of the two sets of animals. Altogether we found that there were at least thirty-six different types of verbs used in the entries. For example, there were verbs such as 'know' and 'think' which in certain contexts indicate degrees of belief; verbal expressions such as 'turn into' and 'convert' which express simple change; others called for the grouping of things, for quantitative values, outcomes of actions, and so on. Promising as this approach appeared to be, it became clear on further analysis that identical verbs occur in questions of quite different logical import. Consider two entries as a case in point: 'What did they decide about the income tax?' and 'Why did you decide on "angrily" as a modifier?'. Both of these entries contain the expression 'did ---- decide.' Yet the first entry asks for a statement of a decision while the second one asks for an explanation as to the use of the word 'angrily.' The number of entries containing the same type of verb or even the same verb, and yet varying in logical significance, made this approach to the formation of categories inadequate.

A second effort to formulate categories consisted in a study of the nouns appearing in entries. It seemed reasonable to suppose that the nature of the nouns would give definite clues to the logical operations required by the entries. For example, the entry 'What is a neuron?' is seen to be quite different from the entry 'What is a felony?' when the nouns 'neuron' and 'felony' are taken into account. A neuron occupies space and is observable; it can be pointed to or described. But a felony is a status ascribed to acts. Acts such as killing, if they occur under certain conditions, are judged to be murder and murder is a felony. Now, killing may be witnessed; it is an observable act. But strictly speaking murder is not observable. For whether killing is murder or not is a matter of decision, usually by a court of law, and not a matter of observation.

Consider also the entry 'What are some characteristics of his writing that you have noticed?'. The central feature of this entry seems to be the term 'characteristics'. Whatever they are, some of them must be designated in order to respond satisfactorily to the entry. Yet what sort of term are we dealing with? Is it the same sort as 'neuron' or 'felony'? 'Characteristics' is a term of great generality. In its widest scope, it is the name of the class of all properties. It denotes a class of terms any member of which may denote the properties of an object. Thus the writing of a given novelist may have a number of properties. It may exhibit a large proportion of metaphors, or great descriptive detail, or lyrical expressions, and so on. Each of these is a property of the writing and is a member of the class of things called characteristics. But the class is not exhausted by the properties of writing, for all properties of all things belong in the class of characteristics. The terms 'relationship' and 'difference,' frequently used in entries, are similar to 'characteristics' with regard to generality.

It follows from the foregoing discussion that nouns may be grouped into sets by levels of abstraction as well as by what they denote. We developed five major sets of nouns based upon the character of their referents and the magnitude of their referential distances.

But, as in the case of our study of verbs, this approach to logical categories had to be abandoned. In the first place, the study of nouns gave no direct clues to logical categories into which entries might be placed. Logical operations, except for definition and classification, are independent of the nouns contained in propositions. This is precisely what one would expect. To deal with nouns, in the foregoing sense, is to analyze a concept. For a noun is the name of a particular object or of a concept, that is, a class of objects. And there is more to logic than the analysis of concepts. In the second place, to distinguish among nouns in logically significant ways is to engage in concept analysis at levels of high abstraction. The inference chain leading from these levels back to the entries themselves is often long and tenuous. For this reason, classification of entries in terms of types of nouns, even were they logically significant, would be of doubtful use.

Another effort to build categories led us to look at the

stems of entries. At the very outset of our efforts to classify
entries it became desirable to group them for convenient handling and
easy reference. This led to the use of entry stems as a basis of
convenient classification. We use 'stem' to refer to the opening word
of an entry, except where entries cannot be usefully grouped by their
opening word. In these cases 'stem' refers to other parts -- usually
the verbs or verb phrases -- of the entry. The following is the way
the entries were thus classified:

1) Verb stems -- Can...? Do...? Have...? Is...? Will...?
   Would...? Let us (with a verb -- have, look, see, etc.)...?

2) Adjective or pronoun stems -- What...? Which...? Who...?

3) Adverb or pronoun stems -- How...? Why...? When...? Where...?

4) Conjunctive stems -- If.... What (when, how, where, etc.)...?

5) Miscellaneous -- Agreement asking (e.g., 'That's the central
   government of Canada, isn't it'); Completion (e.g., 'Our
   conclusion is....'); Complete Declarative (e.g., 'This is
   considered his best novel.'); Imperative (e.g., 'Name some
   words that are negatives.'); Incomplete (e.g., 'For what
   reasons?').

These stems afford only a limited clue to logical categories.
The 'Why...?' and 'How...?' stems, due to their limited linguistic
function, are frequently associated with entries that demand causes,
motives, purposes, ways and means of doing something, and the like.
Likewise, 'If...?' stems are almost always found in entries calling
for conditional reasoning. But other stems are more varied with
respect to the demands made by their entries. For example, 'What...?'
stems are to be found in entries asking for all sorts of logical
responses, as shown in the following entries: 'What is a rhombus?'
'What is the valence of hydrogen?' 'What kind of structure is the
dendron?' 'What equation relates these quantities?' 'What would the
nervous system correspond to in a building?' 'What causes warts?'.
The first of these entries asks for a unique description of a rhombus.
The second one demands that a numerical constant be specified. The
third entry requires that the dendron be classified by its structure.

The next entry calls for the statement of an equation. The next one demands that something about a building that stands in an analogous relation to the nervous system be named. The last of the entries asks that an explanation be given. Yet all these different functions are served by entries having 'What...?' stems. The same sort of variation can be shown, in differing degrees, for other stems. Even the 'How...?' and 'Why...?' stems vary in this regard to some extent. 'How would you define crime?' is logically quite a different entry from 'How would you identify an acid?'. The first of these is not asking for an account of the procedure by which the word 'crime' is defined. Rather it asks that the word be defined. Furthermore, this entry could be understood as asking for a definition of the word 'crime' as used by the person addressed instead of for a dictionary or textbook definition. The second of these entries calls for a procedure by which acids are identified. But, as in the preceding case, the question could be interpreted as asking for the particular procedure used by the person addressed. Because of these variations in the logical demands of entries having the same stem the development of categories by reference to stems did not seem promising.

While the three approaches to the development of logical categories just described failed to yield the desired results, they were not without value. They afforded information about entries which proved to be useful as we turned to the development of criteria. Furthermore, from these approaches we gained a familiarity with certain aspects of entries which reinforced the more intuitive formation of categories to which we now appealed.

As we began to examine a sample set of entries, and to look at each entry as a whole, we became aware of the fact that the logical character of an entry could be decided by reference to the sort of response it demands. This is the approach which we finally used in the development of the categories. When we speak of response, we of course do not mean the response which the student made and which can be found by examining the continuing phase of the episode. Rather, we appeal to an ideal response. Such a response is a schema. It is a

form to which responses to the members of a given class of entries
would conform, regardless of the content with which entries deal, were
the responses logically correct.

The meaning of an ideal response may be further clarified by
reference to examples of entries. The entry 'From which state did Mark
Hanna come?' demands that a particular political unit be specified.
It is not necessary that we know the state from which he came in order
to know that the entry requires as an appropriate response that a
particular state be indicated. Nor do we need to know the time at
which he came from the particular state. Were we asked to give an
actual rather than an ideal response, we would want the ambiguity
removed from the entry by specifying the time. Mark Hanna might have
come from New York, or any one of a number of states, depending upon
the occasion. In the sense of nativity he could have come from one
and only one state. Furthermore, an ideal response may be made in
more than one way. In the present case the particular state could
be specified by naming it, by pointing to it on a map, or by sketching
its shape, and so on. 'Which line is the base of the triangle?' is an
entry which likewise requires that a particular something, namely a
line, be specified. 'What is the word (in the sentence) that is to be
modified?' similarly requires that something -- a word -- be singled
out. We can now generalize what we have been doing and say that there
is a set of entries which demands as a response schema that particular
things be specified by naming, pointing, or whatnot.

In contrast to the foregoing entries are cases in which no
object in particular is called for. From the entry 'What is some food
material that the fish could use?' it is clear that food material is
to be indicated. But the phrase 'some food material' is a variable.
The entry therefore does not demand that a specific food item be
indicated. Any one of a number of foods could be named each of which
would satisfy the demands of the entry equally well. In cases of this
type the response schema consists in naming or otherwise indicating
any one of a number of variables satisfying the function of the entry.

Some entries demand more complex response schemata. 'How
did McKinley happen to be killed?' requires that a sequence of events

leading up to and ending in McKinley's death be related. 'How did they finally relieve this beleaguered garrison?' is an entry which also demands recounting of a chain of events ending in the relief of the garrison. A similar response is to be made to the entry 'In the East, what had Cleveland done that made the Capitalists unhappy?'. Here the response consists in narrating the acts of Cleveland that led to dissatisfaction among the financial leaders. Thus, we have a response schema which consists in the narration of a sequence of events leading up to and culminating in a particular state of affairs. This state of affairs is said to be the result or outcome of the events, and the events are said to explain or to account for the outcome. Again, it is not necessary that we know what the actual events were in order to tell that an entry demands the narration of events as a response.

3. Kinds of Entries

The foregoing discussion is perhaps sufficient to indicate the way in which we arrived at a set of logical categories. The categories into which the entries were grouped are as follows:

1) _Defining_. Entries making up this group are concerned with how words or other symbols are used to refer to objects (abstract or concrete). These entries vary in form and content, but in general they ask implicitly or explicitly for the meaning of terms.

In some cases, a term is given and a definition or meaning of the term is to be supplied as a response to the entry. In the example, 'What does the word "dorsal" mean?', the question requires that whatever is designated by "dorsal" be indicated.

In other cases, neither the word 'mean' nor 'define' occurs in the entry. Rather the entry asks what something _is_, for example, 'What is a cablegram?'. These entries require that the noun appearing in the question be defined, or that the referent of the noun be described.

In a few cases, the noun in the entry is a grammatically proper name. In these cases, the entry requires that the object designated by the proper name be described or otherwise indicated. For example, 'Who was Paul Elmer More?' is a question which asks that the person referred to be described unambiguously.

Finally, some entries ask for a term or expression that can be substituted for another term or expression; for example, 'What is the symbol for gravity?'.

2) <u>Describing</u>. To describe is to represent something by words or drawing, to tell about something. Thus, the entries making up this category mention or suggest something and require that an account of this something be given. In the question 'What can you tell us about the gill rakers?' we are asked to describe the gill rakers.

However, not all questions which mention or allude to something ask for a description. For example, 'What would be some examples of a sense organ?' is a question which names a class of things and asks that instances of it be cited. No description is called for.

In some cases, as in the example just given, it is easy to tell whether the entry requires a description or an identification. But in a large number of entries the intent of the entry in this regard is obscure. 'What did Cleveland find out?' is a question which might be answered by naming whatever it was that Cleveland uncovered. But our expectations would be more nearly satisfied were the question answered by a brief account of what he found out. On the other hand, 'What is a common defect of this part (cerebellum) of the brain?' can plainly be answered by naming the defect. But a description of the defect would not be inappropriate as an answer.

3) <u>Designating</u>. To designate is to identify something by name -- word or other symbol. The name designates the object (abstract or concrete) to which it refers. Thus, this group of entries is made up of items in which something is described or otherwise indicated, and the name used to refer to it or to identify it is asked for. These entries vary widely in form and content. In general, they demand that objects (abstract or concrete) be designated by name or other symbol, or simply by pointing. Consider the question 'What do you call a word used to modify a verb?'. The question is answered by giving the name of the word, namely, 'adverb'. The question 'What reptile did he show in the film?' is answered in the same way, although

the question does not explicitly ask what the reptile is called.
Again, 'What is the word (in a given sentence) that's to be modified?'
is a question which can be answered by pointing to the particular
word or by saying it.

4) <u>Stating</u>. Entries in this group do not ask for names,
descriptions, etc., but for statements of issues, steps in proofs,
rules, obligations, theorems, conclusions, ideas, beliefs, promises,
threats, etc. For example, the question 'What is the conclusion?' asks
for a statement of some sort. It can seldom be answered satisfactorily
merely by naming.

5) <u>Reporting</u>. The entries in this group ask for a report
on what a book or document says, for information in the text, or for
a summary or review, and the like.

6) <u>Substituting</u>. The entries making up this category ask
the student to perform a symbolic operation usually of a mathematical
nature.

7) <u>Evaluating</u>. To engage in evaluating is to estimate the
worth, dependability, etc. of something. An entry of this type requires
that some object, expression, event, action, or state of affairs be
rated as to its value, dependability, desirability, and the like. For
example, the question 'Is he a good judge?' asks the student to rate
a judge who acts in some particular manner.

8) <u>Opining</u>. In opining, the body of evidence from which
the conclusion is drawn is not explicitly delineated by the entry of
the episode, i.e., no explicit conditions are given on which the
conclusion is to be based. The person may be required to supply that
which is the case, or to affirm or deny what is suggested in the entry
as being the case. It is characteristic of such episodes that the
conclusion involves an inference from evidence rather than a report
of a single fact. 'Do you think that historians will say that Wilson
was right in proposing the League of Nations?' is an entry which asks
for a conjecture about how historians of the future will judge Woodrow
Wilson with respect to a particular set of actions -- those involved
in proposing the League of Nations.

9) <u>Classifying</u>. Each entry in this group makes explicit reference to an instance or class (type, sort, group, set, kind) of things or both. The entry requires that a given instance be put in the class to which it belongs, or that a given class be placed in a larger class to which it belongs as a subclass. For example, 'What special type of triangle did you find it to be?' is a question which makes reference by the 'it' to a particular triangle. The student is expected to tell what class of triangles this particular one belongs to. As an illustration of questions which ask that a class be placed in a larger class, consider the following: 'What group of animals does the jellyfish belong to?'. In this question, the term 'jellyfish' does not refer to a particular jellyfish but to a subclass. The student is required to name the larger class to which the group of animals called 'jellyfish' belongs.

10) <u>Comparing and Contrasting</u>. This type of entry requires that two or more things -- actions, factors, objects, processes, etc. -- be compared. In some cases, the entry specifies two or more things, and asks that either their similarities or differences be noted. In other cases, the entry asks that they be compared with respect to a particular characteristic. The question 'What's the difference between probation and parole?' illustrates the first of these cases. The student is asked merely to make a comparison, the points of comparison not being explicitly indicated. The second case is illustrated by the question 'Is his (fish's) eye very large compared to the size of the grasshopper's?'. Here the eyes of the two different animals are to be compared with respect to size only.

In still other cases, the entry names a thing and requires that another thing similar to it, be indicated. Consider the question 'Which one (Canadian house) corresponds to the House of Commons?'. The House of Commons is the given object. The question asks that the Canadian house most like it be named. Entries of this kind do not require that differences or similarities be explicitly stated. The student considers the differences or likenesses and selects the object in terms of them, as required by the entry.

11) <u>Conditional Inferring</u>. These entries contain an antecedent, that is, the conditional part of a statement. In the sentence 'When it rains, the streets are wet' the phrase 'When it rains' is the antecedent. The phrase 'the streets are wet' is the consequent. Now, the entries which make up this category give an antecedent. Sometimes they give both an antecedent and a consequent. But they never contain a consequent alone.

Here is an example of an entry containing an antecedent only: 'How does that (undemocratic handling of colonies) affect the mother country?'. The phrase 'undemocratic handling of colonies' is the antecedent. It describes the condition of which the effect on the mother country is the consequent. The question asks the student to tell what the consequent is. Take another case: 'If that diagonal (in rhombus) is given as 12 and this angle is 60, what is the angle at C and at A?'. The antecedent is 'if that diagonal (in rhombus) is given as 12 and this angle is 60'. The consequent asked for by the question is the size of the angle at C and A. In all cases where the antecedent alone is given, the entry requires that the consequent -- effect, result, outcome, subsequent behavior, etc., -- be supplied as the answer.

Consider an example of an entry containing both an antecedent and a consequent: 'Did you ever get a headache from sleeping in a draft?'. The phrase 'sleeping in a draft' is the antecedent, and 'get a headache' is the consequent. Now, in entries of this sort, the student is required to affirm the consequent, to deny it, or to say he does not know whether he has ever suffered or enjoyed the consequent under the given condition or not.

12) <u>Explaining</u>. There are several types of explanatory entries, but they all have one thing in common. They give a particular consequent and they require that an antecedent be supplied. To explain is to set forth an antecedent condition of which the particular event or process to be explained is taken as the effect, or else, to give the rules, definitions, or facts which are used to justify decisions, judgments, actions, etc. In the example 'Why did the light go out?', the consequent is 'the light go out.' The question asks the student

to give a reason (reasons) to account for the fact that the light is out. The reason(s) is the antecedent.

There are six kinds of explanation entries, depending upon the sort of antecedent used to account for the consequent. They are mechanical, causal, sequent, procedural, teleological, and normative. These are described as follows:

12.1) <u>Mechanical Explaining</u>. This type of entry gives an event or action which is to be accounted for by describing the way the parts of a structure fit or work together. A sample entry will help to make this category clear: 'How (do fish make a sound)?'. The action to be accounted for is 'fish make a sound.' Now, the antecedent consists of some kind of structure which enables the fish to make vibrations. A description of this mechanism would constitute an answer to the entry.

12.2) <u>Causal Explaining</u>. Entries of this type give events, situations, or states to be accounted for and ask that a state of affairs be cited of which the given event (or situation or state) is taken to be the result. Consider the example: 'What makes a person's muscles sort of twitch-like?'. The event to be explained is the twitching of a person's muscles. The explanation consists of a description of the condition of the nerves associated with the twitching.

12.3) <u>Sequent Explaining</u>. Entries of this sort ask how something happened. They require that a sequence of events be cited of which the event to be accounted for is the sequel. For example, the question 'How did McKinley happen to be killed?' requires the recitation of the events leading up to the assassination of President McKinley.

12.4) <u>Procedural Explaining</u>. These entries require that the steps or operations by which a given result or end is attained be described. Here is a sample entry: 'How did you get 72 (for an answer)?'. It is expected that the student tell the steps he took to obtain this answer.

12.5) <u>Teleological Explaining</u>. This type of entry contains descriptions of actions, decisions, states of affairs, or the worth of things. It requires that these be accounted for or justified by reference to purposes, functions, or goals. An entry of this sort is: 'Why are you doing those problems?'. The consequent to be explained is 'doing those problems.' The explanation consists in giving a purpose, say, to satisfy an assignment.

12.6) <u>Normative Explaining</u>. Entries of this type do either of two things. First, they may mention or assume a decision, judgment, or state of knowing and require that it be justified by citing a definition or characteristic or both. Here is an example: '<u>Why do we call them</u> (animals between vertebrates and invertebrates) <u>the Chordata animal group?</u>'. The consequent is the underscored part of the question. To give the antecedent in this case is to cite a definition of the chordata phylum and to point out that the animals in question have the characteristics called for by the definition.

Second, members of this group of entries cite actions, decisions, or choices (either made or to be made) and require that rules be given as reasons for the decisions, choices, etc. Consider this example: 'Why do we use shorter (in comparing two pencils as to length)?'. The consequent to be explained is 'we use shorter.' The antecedent demanded by the question consists of a rule prescribing the use of 'shorter' in such cases. Entries of this type usually call for grammatical or mathematical rules.

13) <u>Directing and Managing Classroom</u>. Many entries have little or no logical significance. They are designed, not to evoke thought, but to keep the classroom activities moving along. Such entries belong in this category.

4. Criteria for Classifying Entries

We turn now to the question of how entries by which episodes are classified are to be placed in the categories set forth in the preceding section. To classify entries it is necessary to satisfy two conditions: first, there must be criteria by which to decide the category into which any entry is to be placed; and, second, these criteria must meet the test of consistency with which different observers, using these criteria, put the same entries into the same categories.

How the Criteria Were Formulated. The criteria were developed from a set of entries taken from a sample of transcripts covering all the subject matter fields represented by the complete set of tapes. There were approximately 1400 entries in the sample set. Each entry was typed on a strip of paper for convenience in handling.

Two investigators, working separately, developed the criteria. They followed the procedure of trial and error. One investigator worked through part of the sample set of entries, putting each entry into the category deemed to be appropriate. The gross experience of classifying entries in this way led to the formulation of a few rules. As other entries were classified, additional rules emerged. When this investigator had worked through the entire set of entries, the rules he had formulated were given to the second investigator who then attempted to classify the entries by the rules. The difficulties encountered by the second investigator were discussed and the tentative criteria were modified to obviate the troubles. By this to and fro exchange between the two workers, the criteria were put into semifinal form. The two investigators, working individually, now classified the entire sample of entries. They then compared their classifications, noting the agreements and disagreements, and making such changes as their deliberations called for. The criteria thus revised were used as the working set.[1]

Reliability of Criteria. The type of reliability estimate used to determine the reliability of the criteria was a coefficient of interjudge agreement, one based on percentage of agreement between independent judgments. The experimental phase involved obtaining independent judgments of a sample of entries. The formula for calculating the coefficient was a rather simple one involving merely frequencies of agreements and disagreements.

Four judges, graduate students in Education at the University of Illinois, were used to obtain the independent judgments required for the reliability test.

Two sample sets of entries were used for the purpose of training the judges. The first was an easy set containing about

---

[1]
    See Appendix 3 for this set of criteria.

55 entries. The other set was more difficult and contained about 120 entries.

Before classifying the first set of entries, the judges were given general instructions and a set of general procedures to be followed in classifying the entries.[2]

After classifying the first set of easy entries independently of each other, the judges met with the staff to check their agreement and to discuss difficulties encountered. The judges then classified the second set of more difficult entries and afterwards met again to check their agreement and to discuss difficulties they encountered.

The final set of about 300 entries was then classified by the judges. The entries in this final set were selected randomly from the entries already classified by the staff. In all but three of the categories -- Defining, Explaining, and Designating -- one out of four entries were selected randomly. In each of the subcategories of Defining and Explaining, one out of three entries were selected randomly, and in the subcategories of Designating one out of four entries were selected randomly. The one exception was Substituting, which had so few entries that they were all used in the final set.

The agreement on this final set of entries was determined for two pairs of judges. This latter procedure was used to minimize the number of sheer oversights likely to occur -- rather than actual misjudgments and misapplications of the criteria. Thus, these coefficients are for pairs of judges, not single judges.[3]

The formula for calculating the coefficient was based upon the number of agreements per category between the two pairs of judges. Thus each category has a separate coefficient.

The formula for this coefficient is: $R_i = \dfrac{A_i}{A_i + D_{1_i} + D_{2_o}}$

where R_i is the coefficient of agreement for category (or subcategory) i; A_i is the number of agreements in category i; D_{1_i} is the number of

---

[2] See Appendix 4 for these instructions and procedures.

[3] It is best that judges always work in pairs rather than singly on this material, because its complexity tends to result in many sheer oversights.

entries placed in category i by the first pair of judges but not by the second pair; and D_{2_i} is the number of entries placed in category i by the second pair of judges but not by the first. The coefficients thus obtained are presented in Table 2.

Table 2. Coefficients of agreement for the criteria
for the logical categories

Name of Category	Coefficient	Name of Category	Coefficient
Defining[4]		Evaluating	.60
(1)	.88		
(2)	.88	Opining	.73
(3)	.33		
(4)	0.00	Classifying	.70
T	.84		
		Comparing & Contrasting	.62
Describing	.67		
		Conditional Inferring	.67
Designating[4]		Explaining	
(1)	.64	(1)	.83
(2)	.62	(2)	.55
(3)	.48	(3)	.36
(4)	.90	(4)	.67
(5)	1.00	(5)	.67
T	.71	(6)	.76
		T	.84
Stating	.63		
Reporting	.33	Directing & Managing Classroom	.87
Substituting	.88		

(The entries designated T -- under Defining, Designating and Explaining -- are for these categories as a whole.)

As can be seen, the coefficients range from 0.00 to 1.00. The median is .67, and the middle 50% of the coefficients range from .62 to .84 -- a fairly high percentage of agreement for the present status of the categories.

Discussion and Interpretation. It seems apparent that much of the unreliability is due to four somewhat distinct types of difficulties.

---

[4] See Appendix 3 for nature of these subcategories.

One type is overlapping between the categories due to the presence of conflicting cues within the entry, i.e., one part of the entry clearly indicates that it is to be placed within one category and another part of the entry clearly indicates that it is to be placed in an entirely different category. Thus disagreement may result from one judge following one cue and another judge following the other cue.

In the second type of difficulty neither the whole entry nor any significant part of the entry seems to satisfy the criteria of any category. When the entry does not seem to belong in any category, judges will disagree as to which of several categories seems to be the most appropriate.

The third type of difficulty is somewhat similar to the first type. It is due to what seems to be a gradual shading of one category into another; e.g., Designating tends to shade into Explanation, the entries seeming to fall along a "continuum." Here judges may differ with respect to the point on the "continuum" at which they separate one category from the other.

The fourth type of difficulty arises from the fact that the criteria involve varying levels of inference, some being extremely high in referential distance from the categories and others very low. The criteria for subcategories (1) and (2) in Defining and (5) in Designating require very little inference. These cases, as already noted, are among the categories high in reliability. It is interesting to note that both verbal and syntactical cues are strong and dependable in the criteria for these categories. The verbal cues 'mean' and 'define' as well as the syntactical cue 'What is X?' go a long way toward indicating unambiguously the category to which entries exhibiting them belong. On the other hand, some categories are marked by criteria requiring a great amount of inference. A case in point is subcategory (2) in Explaining -- Causal Explaining. The criteria in this case are not only vague but they also require the judge to decide whether an entry asks for an explanation of an event, or an explanation of an explanation of an event. Such an interpretation of a criterion, to say the least, involves a high order of reasoning, especially when neither verbal nor syntactical cues are dependable.

It has been possible to develop neither completely independent categories nor suitable criteria by which to eliminate such difficulties, and often it is not clear as to which needs improvement -- the categories or the criteria.

Chapter IV

LOGICAL OPERATIONS: THEIR OCCURRENCE AND DISTRIBUTION

This chapter will present the results we have obtained up to
this point with the logical categories. We will first treat the actual
existence and relative frequency of logical operations in teaching
behavior, and then discuss briefly differences in the occurrence of
these operations among schools, grade levels, and content areas --
Mathematics, Science, Social Studies, English, and Core Program.

It should be emphasized that the analysis at this point is
of the sheer frequency of the logical demands as they appear in the
entries. We have not as yet analyzed the sequences or patterns of
these demands, nor the ways in which they are handled within the bodies
of the episodes. However, the latter analysis is taken up later,
beginning in the next chapter.

1. Logical Operations in Teaching

The purpose of this first phase of our investigation, as
indicated earlier, was to determine what logical patterns, if any, are
to be found in teaching. To accomplish this end, all entries were
classified by the two members of the project staff (the principal
investigators) who were responsible for developing the categories.
Each entry was placed in one and only one category, no disagreements
being permitted. The distribution of entries by logical categories
obtained by this procedure is presented in Table 3. The classes have
been grouped by subject matter and content areas.

It is clear from examining Table 3 that several distinct
types of logical operations are present in teaching behavior. Not only
are there different logical operations, but they differ in the frequency
with which they occur. There is no clearly appropriate method for
obtaining expected frequencies in each of the categories from our data,
nor do we have any defensible rational basis for determining the
expected frequencies in each category. Therefore, we have not employed

a significance test to establish that these categories vary in frequency of occurrence. However, with such a large number of entries, it seems doubtful that any statistical test is required to support the conclusion that the number of entries varies significantly from one category to another. Describing, Designating (3T), and Explaining (12T) are the three most frequently occurring operations in that order, with Directing and Managing Classroom and Conditional Inferring and Stating next. The least frequent operations, aside from subcategories, are Substituting, Reporting, and Classifying. We conclude, then, that we have established that there are logical operations in teaching, and furthermore that some of these operations are more prevalent than others, notably Describing, Designating, and Explaining, in that order.

2. Logical Operations and Content Areas

As shown in Table 3, there are marked differences from class to class in the frequencies of the logical operations. Although the analysis and interpretation of such differences is not central to this study, and was not included in its original purpose and design, some discussion of these differences might be of interest. Since the data were not gathered for the purpose of clarifying the relative effects of teachers, subjects, schools, and grade levels on the nature and frequency of logical operations, these variables are highly confounded. Thus the following discussion is quite speculative.

The schools differ with respect to money expenditure per student, sociocultural characteristics, etc. Such differences would probably influence the logical demands in the classroom mostly through the medium of the teacher, so that school differences probably reduce to differences in teachers. Thus, for the purpose of this discussion, we will ignore differences among schools.

The classes vary from the ninth to the twelfth grades. This variation in grade level, however, occurs in an age range in which the capacity of the average student to handle logical demands probably is roughly the same from one age level to another. On the basis of a great deal of evidence concerning the development of IQ with maturation,

Table 3. Distribution of Logical Categories by Areas and Subjects.

	Mathematics	Science				Social Studies #				
Area → Subject	Geometry	Physics	Chemistry	Biology	Physiology	U.S. History$_B$	U.S. History$_E$	U.S. History$_A$	World History	Sociology
Category										
1. Defining										
1.11	5	2	3	7	11	2	2	0	10	6
1.12	4	1	2	4	14	4	0	0	7	1
1.13	0	0	0	0	0	2	4	0	0	0
1.14	0	10	2	0	1	1	0	0	0	0
1T*	9	13	7	11	26	9	6	0	17	7
2. Describing	97	63	59	110	62	39	82	13	49	35
3. Designating										
3.11	1	0	8	17	11	2	2	0	1	12
3.12	4	1	1	7	6	1	4	0	2	0
3.13	29	7	11	28	27	6	4	1	4	6
3.14	0	0	0	0	14	13	40	8	42	3
3.15	2	2	0	13	6	1	4	0	5	2
3T*	36	10	20	65	64	23	54	9	54	23
4. Stating	58	12	7	5	5	10	16	2	4	4
5. Reporting	6	7	0	9	14	5	6	0	9	13
6. Substituting	4	4	0	0	0	0	0	0	0	2
7. Evaluating	2	4	13	1	4	23	4	2	17	7
8. Opining	6	1	5	3	12	43	27	6	5	8
9. Classifying	11	2	6	20	2	2	4	1	2	2
10. Comparing and Contrasting	11	8	5	23	7	7	6	3	6	5
11. Conditional Inferring	37	26	15	22	19	12	9	2	25	16
12. Explaining										
12.1 Mechanical	0	1	0	12	6	0	0	0	0	0
12.2 Causal	0	6	8	11	14	18	7	3	12	9
12.3 Sequent	0	0	0	5	0	9	17	0	4	2
12.4 Procedural	16	3	10	4	4	0	4	0	4	1
12.5 Teleological	2	0	2	4	5	12	6	4	4	4
12.6 Normative	22	0	6	11	1	8	2	0	2	4
12T*	40	10	26	47	30	47	36	7	26	20
13. Directing and Managing Classroom	39	6	17	12	15	49	7	8	29	9
Total number of entries per subject	356	166	180	328	260	269	257	53	243	151

*Indicates total number of entries in this category.

#Subscripts on the subjects in this area indicate the school in which this class was taped.

Table 3 - Continued

Area →	English ⌐			Core Program		
Subject → Category	English 9	English 11	English 12	Core Program	Number of entries in the category	Percent of total number of entries
1. Defining						
1.11	11	4	6	0	69	2.0
1.12	1	0	6	0	44	1.3
1.13	1	0	3	0	10	0.3
1.14	0	1	0	1	16	0.5
1T*	13	5	15	1	139	4.1
2. Describing	39	40	15	77	861	25.3
3. Designating						
3.11	15	2	0	0	71	2.1
3.12	7	1	0	0	34	1.0
3.13	38	8	9	14	192	5.7
3.14	2	16	8	4	150	4.4
3.15	6	10	3	3	57	1.7
3T*	68	37	20	21	504	14.8
4. Stating	94	2	7	4	230	6.8
5. Reporting	6	0	6	18	99	2.9
6. Substituting	0	0	0	0	10	0.3
7. Evaluating	7	19	44	9	156	4.6
8. Opining	3	11	37	12	179	5.3
9. Classifying	21	12	11	7	103	3.0
10. Comparing and Contrasting	8	10	11	2	112	3.3
11. Conditional Inferring	9	17	24	15	248	7.3
12. Explaining						
12.1 Mechanical	0	0	1	1	21	0.6
12.2 Causal	4	2	17	3	114	3.4
12.3 Sequent	2	6	4	0	49	1.4
12.4 Procedural	4	3	4	5	62	1.8
12.5 Teleological	4	6	21	5	79	2.3
12.6 Normative	44	4	8	1	113	3.3
12T*	58	21	55	15	438	12.9
13. Directing and Managing Classroom	38	18	22	49	318	9.4
Total Number of entries per subject	364	192	348	230	3397	

---

* Indicates total number of entries in this category.
⌐ Subscripts on the subjects in this area indicate the grade level of the class.

it seems that there is little significant increase in the IQ beyond
the ninth grade; thus the capacity of the student to handle intellectual operations probably changes very little during the high school
years. Also, Piaget's observations have led him to conclude that the
handling of propositional logic has been achieved by most normal
adolescents by the time they have reached high school. Thus, for the
purposes of this discussion, we can ignore not only the differences
in schools but the differences in grade levels insofar as maturation
of the student is a factor in determining the logical operations at
these levels.

However, these assumptions still leave the teacher and
subject matter variables confounded. It is unrealistic to assume that
neither of these variables has little or no effect on the distribution
of logical operations. It is plausible to suspect that teachers will
differ in the extent to which they employ different logical operations.
Consider two U.S. history classes at the eleventh-grade level that
dealt with fairly similar historical periods, labeled in Table 3 as
U.S. history$_B$ and U.S. history$_E$. In the U.S. history$_B$ class, there
are fewer entries especially in Describing, the 3.14 subcategory of
Designating, and Sequent Explaining, but there are more entries in
Evaluating, Opining, Causal Explaining, and Directing and Managing
Classroom. These differences seem to be attributable to the teachers'
ways of handling the material, rather than to differences in the
subject matter.

It is also quite plausible that there are differences from
subject to subject within a content area (e.g., physics vs. biology
in the science area), and from one content area to another. Although
we realize that the teacher and subject variables are confounded, we
shall summarize what seem to be the main differences between the
classes within and among the content areas. These might indicate to
some extent -- to what extent cannot be determined from our data --
differences among the subjects and areas with respect to the frequency
with which the various logical operations occur.

Differences within Content Areas. Within both the mathematics and core program areas there is only one subject, thus permitting

no comparisons within these areas.

Within the science area, physiology is more concerned with Defining (1.12) and Designating (3.13) than the other subjects; physics is concerned more with the use of symbols (1.14) and Conditional Inferring; biology and chemistry deal more with Evaluating (correctness of evidence, correct answers to problems, etc.) than either physics or physiology. It is interesting also to note that little difference among the subjects appears in three of the Explaining subcategories (Causal, Sequent, and Teleological); differences do appear in Mechanical Explaining, where biology is especially high; in Procedural Explaining, where chemistry is high; and in Normative Explaining, where biology is especially high, probably because of its emphasis on justifying classifications.

In social studies, sociology is somewhat high in 3.11, but is low in 3.14, as is U.S. history$_B$. On the other hand, U.S. history$_E$ is high on 3.14, as is world history. U.S. history$_B$ is quite high on Opining, but world history is low in this category. U.S. history$_B$ is also very high on Directing and Managing Classroom. This is probably due to the "student-centered" characteristics of this class. World history and sociology are slightly high on Conditional Inferring; U.S. history is somewhat low in this category.

In the English courses, the ninth-grade class was mainly concerned at the time with the learning and application of rules of grammar, whereas the eleventh- and twelfth-grade classes were occupied at the time with topics in literature, involving discussions of novels, etc. These content differences were reflected in the distribution of entries in the logical categories. The concern with the statement and justification of the use of grammatical rules resulted in many entries in Stating and Normative Explaining, whereas the discussion of characters and issues in the novels resulted in many entries in the Opining and Evaluating categories.

Differences among Content Areas. Table 4 contains the number of entries in each category organized by the area. The main differences among the areas appears in Stating, two designating subcategories (3.13,

Table 4. Distribution of Logical Categories by Areas

Category	Area → Mathe-matics	Science	Social Studies	English	Core	Number of entries in the category	% of total number of entries
1. Defining							
1.11	5	23	20	21	0	66	2.0
1.12	4	21	12	7	0	44	1.3
1.13	0	0	6	4	0	10	0.3
1.14	0	13	1	1	1	16	0.5
1T*	9	57	39	33	1	139	4.1
2. Describing	97	294	218	175	77	861	25.3
3. Designating							
3.11	1	36	17	17	0	71	2.1
3.12	4	15	7	8	0	34	1.0
3.13	29	73	21	55	14	192	5.7
3.14	0	14	106	26	4	150	4.4
3.15	2	21	12	19	3	57	1.7
3T*	36	159	163	125	21	504	14.8
4. Stating	58	29	36	103	4	230	6.8
5. Reporting	6	30	33	12	18	99	2.9
6. Substituting	4	4	2	0	0	10	0.3
7. Evaluating	2	22	53	70	9	156	4.6
8. Opining	6	21	89	51	12	179	5.3
9. Classifying	11	30	11	44	7	103	3.0
10. Comparing and Contrasting	11	43	27	29	2	112	3.3
11. Conditional Inferring	37	82	64	50	15	248	7.3
12. Explaining							
12.1 Mechanical	0	19	0	1	1	21	0.6
12.2 Causal	0	39	49	23	3	114	3.4
12.3 Sequent	16	5	32	12	0	49	1.4
12.4 Procedural	2	21	9	11	5	62	1.8
12.5 Teleological	22	11	30	31	5	79	2.3
12.6 Normative	40	18	16	56	1	113	3.3
12T*	39	113	136	134	15	438	12.9
13. Directing and Managing Classroom	0	50	102	78	49	318	9.4
Total number of entries in area	356	934	973	904	230	3397	

* Indicates total number of entries in this category.

3.14), two Explaining subcategories (Mechanical and Normative),
Directing and Managing Classroom, Opining, and Evaluating. In these
categories, science is especially low in Stating, a Designating subcategory (3.14), Normative Explaining, Opining, Evaluating, and Directing and Managing Classroom; it is high in Mechanical Explaining and a
Designating subcategory (3.13). The pattern for social studies is
exactly the reverse of science except for Normative Explaining (where
both areas are low). Both mathematics and English are high in Stating and Normative Explaining, whereas English is high and mathematics
low in Opining and Evaluating.

We may conclude tentatively from this brief discussion, then,
that it seems likely that differences may exist in the extent to which
the logical operations are employed from teacher to teacher, and from
area to area. Adequate answers as to what this extent is, however,
cannot be determined from our data, but await further studies designed
more specifically to investigate these matters.

PART TWO

Chapter V

ANALYSIS OF EPISODES: INTRODUCTION

For pedagogical purposes it is not sufficient to know that
logical operations are used in teaching. In addition, it is important
to know the structure of these operations and the rules by which the
quality of their performance can be decided; to know, for example,
the essential elements of the explanatory pattern of behavior and how
these elements are related to one another in such a way as to constitute a complete explanatory operation. The task to be dealt with in
the following chapters is to analyze each of the major categories of
episodes into subcategories and to set forth the operations they
involve together with the rules by which they are governed.

1. Basis of Analysis

In our initial analysis of episodes we sorted them into
categories by reference to the ideal responses required by entries.
To do the more detailed analysis which we are now undertaking we
focused on actual responses in the episode's continuing phase. By
considering the responses each major category was analyzed into subsets.

In making this further analysis we used a number of
approaches. In the first place, we approached the analysis of episodes
in Conditional Inferring, Explaining, Opining, Evaluating, Defining,
and Designating from the standpoint of two closely related factors:
first, the logical relations between the entry and the response to it,
and second, the rules of correctness or justification. It should be
noted that we are not here concerned with the logical relations
between the entry and an ideal response to the entry, but rather with
the relation between the entry and the actual response which was made
to it. The rules of correctness or justification, however, have
reference to an ideal relationship between the two.

These two factors are very closely related. In categories
such as Defining and Designating, where the emphasis is typically on

the relation between a term and its referent, the classifications
seem to rest largely on structural relations between terms and
referents, and the rules of correctness all seem to be conventions.
On the other hand, in categories such as Conditional Inferring and
Explaining, there is more of a balance between the two factors. In
fact, it is difficult to separate the two: the kind of relation
determines the kind of rule, and the kind of rule helps identify the
logical relation. Thus the role of each factor in deciding upon subsets within the major categories is difficult to identify.

Consider two categories as examples. In conditional
inferring episodes the classification of responses is based primarily
on the kinds of rules and principles used in justification of the
inference. The inference may be logically necessary; it may follow by
a grammatical rule; or it may be justified by an empirical correlation
between relevant variables, etc. The corresponding logical relations
are analytic, deductive, inductive, etc. In evaluating episodes the
responses are classified on the basis of the kind of criteria or
justification given for the evaluation. The evaluation may be supported
by rules, by a comparison with some accepted standard, or merely by the
respondent's personal feelings or preferences. These rules and
standards of comparison, too, have corresponding logical relations but
these relations are not adequately described in philosophical or other
literature.

In the second place, we approached the analysis of episodes
in Classifying and Comparing-Contrasting from a different angle. The
subcategories in Classifying have been based upon the kinds of questions
which students are asked rather than upon the criteria by which classifications are made. If teachers and students engaged in complete
operations of classification, there would be good reason to look more
closely at the different sorts of criteria which are employed in the
classificatory operation. An examination of these criteria would
doubtless yield a different way of developing subsets of classificatory
operations. But when our observations are limited to what teachers are
actually doing in the classroom, it seems more to the point to use a
basis of classification which would make explicit the kind of behavior
which the teacher calls for in the classificatory category.

The same course of reasoning has led us to work out sub-categories of Comparison-Contrast in terms of the question of whether or not there is a standard of comparison given in the entries of the episodes. We have not examined the criterial basis of the acts of comparing and contrasting, but on the contrary have looked at the episodes from the standpoint of whether or not a standard or basis was given for the comparison or contrast. It would seem that the operation of comparing and contrasting where a standard is given would be a different operation than in cases where a standard is not given.

Since the analysis of major categories into subsets is still rather tentative, and no formal criteria for subsets have been developed, we have conducted no reliability studies to establish the dependability of the analyses and classifications presented in the following chapters. In a number of chapters we indicate briefly what some alternative modes of classification might be, having tried and discarded them as less significant than the approaches described herein.

2. Development of Epistemic Rules

A logical operation not only exhibits a structure but it also involves rules. Indeed, there is a sense in which the performance of a logical operation can be said to be rule-guided behavior. Some rules have reference to how the operations should be performed; some deal with the validity; and some with empirical dependability. Roughly speaking, there are three classes of logical rules: those concerning logical validity, those concerning truth, and those concerning correctness. We call those which have to do with correctness epistemic rules. We chose to develop epistemic rules, because these include the other two and because the concept of correctness is comprehensive enough to assess many responses for which the concepts of validity and truth are either irrelevant or extend far beyond their normal domain. For example, one does not typically speak of a true description, but rather of a correct or accurate description.

Although epistemic rules are in most cases appropriate for assessing the correctness of responses, some do not seem to be governed or appraisable in terms of such rules. This is especially true of responses for episodes in the 'Appeal to Personal Factors' subcategory, in Evaluating, and episodes in the 'Description by Giving Personal Impressions' subcategory in Describing. These responses involve reporting one's feelings, preferences, impressions, sensations, etc. The correctness of these reports cannot be determined objectively.

It is interesting to speculate briefly about the role of rules in teaching. The teacher's authority for saying that a student's response is either correct or incorrect has traditionally rested largely upon what the textbook says. This practice has been decried as enslaving the student and the teacher intellectually, as thwarting initiative and creativity, and as emphasizing memorization in learning. If this practice is to be abandoned, it would seem that the teacher must learn to understand and control the logical operations which he and his students perform. The responses given by the student are correct because of what the book says or they are correct on logical grounds. Of course, they may be correct on both counts. But the teacher who is able to move about logically in a network of ideas and to monitor the performance of logical operations would appear to be free, in large measure, from enslavement to the text. To monitor such performance the teacher must have recourse to the rules by which logical operations may be evaluated. To be sure it is not necessary that the teacher be constantly aware of the rules which he is using as he evaluates the performance of logical operations in the classroom. But he should be able to refer to such rules when the need for doing so arises.

To develop epistemic rules we used two procedures. One was to survey logical and philosophical literature for relevant rules already worked out, e.g., on definition, classification, and explanation. The second procedure was to formulate rules outright, by starting with a formulation thought to be logically adequate to handle a few episodes in a category, then to search for counterexamples to the formulation, and finally to modify the formulation of the rule in terms of both the counterexamples and the rules already formulated.*

One important distinction should be kept in mind while using or evaluating the rules we have proposed, i.e., the distinction between a rule and a rule-formulation. A rule-formulation is a particular linguistic expression of the rule, such as might be given in a particular imperative sentence, e.g., 'Don't use negative definitions.'. The rule itself is expressed in or by the sentence -- the rule-formulation -- but the rule is not the sentence itself. If the rule were the sentence, then each different way of saying the rule would constitute a different rule. This distinction is similar to the well-known distinction between a proposition and a sentence expressing the proposition. Thus, in using or evaluating the epistemic rules we have proposed, one should keep in mind that these are actually rule-formulations and concentrate on abstracting the sense of a particular formulation. In spite of the importance of the distinction, however, for convenience and simplicity of style we shall use the term 'rule' where it is actually correct to use the term 'rule-formulation.'

One further point on the nature of epistemic rules is in order. These rules are concerned with appraising or assessing a response in terms of its correctness. The rules are not to be construed either as describing the way a response is formulated (e.g., the psychological processes involved) or as describing the response itself. Of course, this is not to say that there is no connection whatsoever between the formulation of a response and its assessment, or between the description of a response and its assessment. But whatever relation may obtain in either case is unknown or at least not very clear.

Another class of rules are non-logical in character, and are concerned with relations between the responses and persons uttering or receiving the responses. These are called pragmatic rules. They deal with such matters as persuasive order of logical elements (evidence,

---

* The formulation of the classifications did not involve distinctions between teacher and student utterances. Usually the student answers the entry, but many times it will be the teacher who answers it. The teacher may modify, elaborate, clarify, etc., or even completely answer the entry himself.

premises, warrants, etc.), intelligibility of responses, comprehension
of listeners, etc. Since the development of sound pragmatic rules
would involve experimental work, it is beyond the scope of this
project.

3. Relations among Categories

Our original conception of the classes of entries was that
they were to be distinct kinds of logical categories, with no relations
among them. We soon found, however, that such was not the case. The
following general remarks are intended to indicate briefly the nature
of some of these relations.

In our work on the entry categories, we encountered several
kinds of phenomena which suggested inadequacies in our conception.
For one thing, none of the categories was homogeneous, i.e., all the
ideal responses to entries in the category were not of one logical
type. The most non-homogeneous were Defining, Describing, Designating,
and Explaining. Three of these had logically distinct subcategories,
and Describing was so heterogeneous we did not even try to establish
logically distinct subcategories.

Secondly, there seemed to be different kinds of relations
among the entry categories, some coming from similarity of linguistic
cues in the entry, others from similarities or contrasts in the ideal
responses required by the entry. Consider the following examples of
the various relations. The relation between Defining and Designating
is a kind of inverse relation in the logical elements supplied in the
entry as opposed to those required in the ideal response. In Defining,
the logical element supplied is the term, and the ideal response
required is the referent of the term. In Designating, the logical
element supplied is the referent, and the ideal response required is
the corresponding term. On the other hand, the relation between
Describing and Explaining is in a sense one of indistinguishability of
the linguistic cues in the entry over a range of contexts. In these
contexts an entry may be considered, e.g., as either requiring an
explanation or a description. Changes in the wording of the entry

may or may not change the nature of the logical operation required. The same kind of indistinguishability arises between the entries requiring opining about something and those requiring evaluating in terms of a personal set of criteria. Still another kind of relation is one in which it seems that one logical operation is a means to, is assumed by, or is a part of, another operation. We classify something in order to describe it, or we describe something in order to explain it. Or, in terms of assumptions, designating assumes no other operation, describing assumes only designating and classifying.

In the analyses to be presented in the following chapters, the reader is likely to detect further relations, especially those between the logical elements (consequent, antecedent, etc.) supplied in the entry and logical elements given in the response. These relations differ depending upon whether "reasoning" or "term-referent" categories are involved. Three of these relations will be indicated briefly -- the first two are well known and involve the "reasoning" categories: Explaining, Conditional Inferring, Evaluating, and Opining. The first is an analytic or conventional relation. We find these in Normative Explaining, Analytic Conditional Inferring, and Application of Logical Rules in Evaluating. Second is an empirical or inductive relation. We find these in Empirical-Subsumptive Explaining and in Empirical Conditional Inferring. It is often involved in Evaluating by Consequences. The third is a judgmental relation. We find this in Evaluating by Comparison with a Standard, the Opining category, the Executive Conditional Inferring, and Judgmental Explaining. In each of these it will be seen that judgment plays an important role determining whether criteria apply in a particular case, in deciding the best way to do something, and so forth. Much work needs to be done to clarify the nature of the epistemic rules when judgmental relations are involved.

There are not only relations among the main logical categories but also among the subdivisions of almost every one of these main categories. For example, in Evaluating, it is not always easy to distinguish the subcategories of Application of Rules and Comparison with a Standard. In borderline cases a standard may be so clear and widely accepted that the use of it seems like applying a rule; or a rule may be sufficiently vague in application to a particular thing being evaluated that the rule operates somewhat as a standard. However, the two kinds of evaluating are quite distinct in so many instances that the distinction is a very useful one, if not always clear-cut.

Still further relations -- those between the entry subcategories, described in Chapter III, and the response subcategories to be presented in the following chapters -- have not yet been worked out. There will be some discrepancy, of course, because the entry subcategories were developed partly on the basis of differences among linguistic cues in the entry and such differences would not necessarily be reflected in the responses.

4. Miscellanea

The following considerations have to do with the presentation of episodes as typical examples of subcategories, the frequency and occurrence of subcategories, and the omission of certain categories.

Presentation of episodes. Episodes used as examples of subcategories will be presented with a brief description of the episode's context, and a short discussion of the episode to clarify how it exemplifies the subcategory. The method of analysis consists in describing and illustrating a model of each type of episode together with the epistemic rules for its appraisal. Then such variations of these models as are found in classroom discourse are presented and discussed.

As episodes are presented, they are discussed from the standpoint of how well they measure up to models of the particular operation. For example, in discussing the operation of Explaining it is pointed out that typically the explanatory principle is omitted in classroom discussion. Likewise it is noted that the criterial basis of the value judgment is typically ignored in classroom discourse. It should be understood that these are logical criticisms. They do not represent any evaluation of the teaching from a pedagogical standpoint. Whether or not teaching behavior would have more desirable effects were it to conform more closely to logical models is an empirical question which this study is not designed to answer. All that we are here concerned to do is to make a logical analysis of the teaching operations we have identified. Furthermore, we have ignored factual and other substantive errors which sometimes occur in the rush of verbal exchanges in the classroom. Since these errors do not affect the logical analysis, we have made no effort to correct or to call attention to them in our analysis of episodic material.

Frequency of occurrence. Because we have no data on the reliability of the classifications, we have not reported or even calculated any frequency distributions. Of course, we have noticed that some of the subcategories are represented by few episodes. This may or may not turn out to be a stable finding, but at present could be attributed to sampling error.

Omission of categories. Four of the main categories -- Substituting, Reporting, Stating, and Describing -- are not dealt with in the following chapters. Substituting has been omitted because the number of episodes in this category is too small to warrant an analysis of it. Reporting and Stating have comparatively little logical and pedagogical significance. Since it was necessary to conserve time, we decided to forego further analysis of these categories.

Describing turned out to be an extremely complex category. It became clear that a complete analysis of it would require far more time than was available to us in this phase of the work. We did, however, analyze about 50 out of the approximately 850 Describing episodes.

Five subcategories were developed, which, with further analysis, might turn out to have some logical significance. These may be characterized and illustrated briefly as follows. (1) Description by characterization. This involves explicit mention of at least one significant characteristic of the thing to be described: President

Jackson was a high-tempered man with firm convictions. (2) Description by verbal identification. This occurs when the thing to be described is in some sense equated with another item: the year the British used rockets against Americans is equated with the year 1812. (3) Description by purpose. Here a thing is described by giving its purpose, function, or intention: the purpose of the first satellite was to check the atmosphere. (4) Description by assigning numerical value. This involves selecting a quantifiable feature of the thing to be described and assigning a number to the feature: the circumference of the satellite was about 40 inches. (5) Description by giving personal impressions. Here something is usually described by giving a cognitive-affective reaction to the thing: one's impression of John Adams as a man of principle is described as liking him, thinking he was pretty good, etc.

Chapter VI

DEFINING EPISODES

A defining episode is one in which the teacher gives the
meaning of a term or expression or attempts to elicit its meaning
from students.

The definitions in defining episodes serve a number of
purposes. It is difficult to identify a teacher's purpose in an
episode, but an interpretation of an episode in the context of its
occurrence usually gives some insight into why the definition is
introduced at that particular point in classroom discussion. There
are some four different purposes for definitions. First, they are
introduced to express a concept which has been developed already.
When definitions are used in this way, they are usually summary statements intended to pin down a concept in verbal form. In the second
place, definitions are used to set the grounds of discussion. They
serve as a frame of reference in terms of which to make subsequent
remarks. This use of definitions is found rather infrequently. In
the third place, definitions are used in developing concepts and are
intended as a way of clarifying concepts which would otherwise be
vague. Finally, definitions are introduced as a way of reviewing
previous discussion or to check the students' understanding of a
concept or of how a word is used.

A definition is a sentence which is intended to convey the
meaning of a term. The term to be defined is usually the name of a
concept, so that the definition of a term is the verbal expression of
the concept for which the term stands. In other words, the psychological counterpart of a definition is a concept. Of course, a
definition does not exhaust a concept. A linguistic expression never
exhausts its subject matter, and this is doubtless the case in any
effort to express a concept. No matter how refined and extended the
definition may be, there is always something left unsaid with respect
to the concept being expressed. Nevertheless, concepts can be handled,

clarified, refined, and made more precise through efforts to express them linguistically.

An analysis of defining episodes will indicate the ways in which teachers use words to express or clarify concepts. There is a number of ways of expressing concepts, and, while a definition is not the only way in which concepts may be exhibited in behavior, they do constitute the usual modes of expressing them.

We have identified five different types of definitions: (a) exemplary definitions, (b) equivalence definitions, (c) proper name definitions, (d) classificatory definitions, and (e) relational definitions.

1. Exemplary Definition

This type is one in which one or more examples of the referent of the term to be defined are indicated.

Model of Exemplary Definition

Term or expression $\longrightarrow$ An instance of what-
to be defined ever the term is
used to stand for

The rules governing the appraisal of exemplary definitions are as follows:

    a. The example must either be pointed to or unambiguously denoted verbally.

    b. An instance must be one which authorities would accept as an example.

This type of definition is best illustrated by a situation in which an individual points to an actual instance as an example of what the term to be defined refers to. Suppose a person asks: "What is a J-tube?" and someone says to him, "Here, this is a J-tube" (pointing to such a tube as he speaks). When pointed to, the referent of the term 'J-tube' is apt to be unmistakable. In classroom situations, the reference to examples is seldom made by pointing, but often by mentioning them. Furthermore, the instances which are mentioned are frequently processes or abstract categories rather than concrete objects or events. Here are some episodes illustrative of exemplary definition.

*

Episode 1 T: What is meant by straight thinking?

      S: Like during an emergency, knowing what to do.

      T: Yes, that would be some straight thinking.

*

Knowing-what-to-do-in-an-emergency is cited as an instance of straight thinking. The example consists in a disposition rather than observable behavior.

    Another example is as follows.

*

Episode 2 T: What do we mean by moralizing?

      S: It means.... (student's remark unclear)

      T: It bothers her -- would you say? What do we mean by moralizing? If I come in every morning and I say, "Students, this is our thought for today: 'Do unto others as you would have them do unto you' -- this is one thought; and 'a penny saved is a penny earned,' and then I say, 'always be good because goodness pays off'," am I moralizing?

      S: Yes.

      T: Or, if I'm talking all the time -- and I say, "all right, let's stop here. Here is this man, this just goes to show you that dishonesty is an evil thing" then, I am moralizing. When I take an example and make a rule to live by from it when I comment on life and say, "this is the way it is" -- a certain way, that I'm moralizing, am I not? I'm giving you a set of morals, in a way, to live by. Now, Graham Greene does this, I think, but he does it well, to me in such a good way that I agree with him, and I don't find this offensive.
        I'll show you just an example of this so that you'll know what you are looking for when I say "moralizing influences" or "moralizing sentences". Maybe that's not the best way for it, but look on page 50. He says, this is Scobie's attitude, you see, and we get the feeling it might be Graham Greene's attitude too,

because he's so consistent throughout the book
when he said -- it's the last sentence, about
three -- about seven lines up, the end of the
line: "Despair is the price one pays for setting
oneself an impossible aim. It is, one is told,
the unforgivable sin, but it is a sin that the
corrupt or evil man never practices. He always
has hope. He never reaches the breaking point of
knowing absolute failure. It's always a man of
good will who carries always in his heart a
capacity for damnation." Now, don't you feel
this is a kind of moralizing? This is a
setting of criticism of society down for us to
accept. I don't think it's bad but it seems to
me it's quite well done and quite full of....
but as you read through these pages here, see if
you find other examples of this because I'll ask
you for them, and since you are looking for them,
maybe you'll find too many. I don't know, but
they are quite prevalent. On every other page or
so you will find one of these criticisms of life,
which to me seem pretty interesting.

*

Note that the teacher is giving a number of instances of the way in
which a person might moralize, using himself as a possible example.
Then he goes ahead to indicate that Graham Greene moralizes over and
over again in the pages of the novel. In order to find out whether or
not the students have understood what is meant by the term 'moralizing',
the teacher asks the students to identify sentences which could be
interpreted as moralizing. The supposition is that if the students
can identify sentences as moralizing, and if the sentences they identify
are the same as those which the teacher himself would identify, then
they have understood the meaning of the term, or at least they have
the beginnings of the concept of moralizing. In this episode we see
an instance of how a teacher attempts to build a concept by citing
examples.

Another case of this type of definition is illustrated in
the following episode.

*

Episode 3   S: What does the word 'spoils' refer to?

S_2: It... what it really means is, the person who
wins gets to appoint a friend.

*

An example of the kind of behavior -- appointing a friend by a person elected to office -- manifested under the Spoils System is given to indicate the meaning of the term.

2. Verbal Equivalence Definition

This type of definition is one in which a synonym or synonymous expression of the term to be defined is given.

Model of Verbal Equivalence Definition

Term to be defined	⟶	A word or expression having the same or nearly the same meaning as the word or expression to be defined

The rules for the appraisal of verbal equivalence definitions are as follows:

a. The equivalent term must have a meaning approximately the same as that of the term being defined.

b. The equivalent term must have an established meaning, and not simply used for the occasion.

c. The context for understanding the term being defined together with the equivalent term can be taken for granted.

The following episodes represent definitions which correspond to the model set forth above.

*

Episode 4   S: What is sentiment?

         T: Sentiment means sympathy, doesn't it?

*

Episode 5   T: The P-L-E 'principle' means what?

         S: Rule.

         T: A rule, a theory, an idea.

*

Episode 6   T: What is mental fatigue?

         S: It is when you can't think straight or you're tired. Your brain is tired.

T: Well, it would be from the -- tired brain.

S: Tired brain?

T: Yes, from thinking or reading or doing mental work.

*

These cases may be reduced to the above model, as follows:

Sentiment $\longrightarrow$ Sympathy

Principle $\longrightarrow$ Rule, theory, idea

Mental fatigue $\longrightarrow$ Tired brain

In the first case, the word sentiment is not understood by the student. The teacher assumes that the term 'sympathy' is perhaps better understood, and offers it as having an equivalent meaning. The same analysis holds for Episode 5. The meaning of 'principle' is made clear by reference to such familiar terms as 'rule', 'theory', and 'idea'. Of course, had the students been asked to give the meaning of these terms, they would perhaps have been somewhat at a loss to do so. They know in general their meanings. But they would probably not be able to give any precise definition of these terms. Nevertheless, in this situation the teacher thought it sufficient merely to give the synonymous terms without any elaboration. In Episode 6, the expression 'tired brain' is perhaps understood in the same sort of way as the terms 'rule', 'theory', and 'idea'. The students have some familiarity with what it means to be tired and they simply transfer the meaning from muscular fatigue with which they are familiar to mental fatigue. Yet the meaning of the term 'mental fatigue' in a precise sense is certainly not given in the equivalent expression 'tired brain'.

It is clear from these examples that equivalent definitions tend to shade off in the direction of vagueness, and sometimes the equivalent terms are so vague that the students do not know what the meaning of the term being defined really is. The following example will give some indication of this sort of vagueness.

*

Episode 7   S: What is a tariff wall?

T: All right, both sides have tariffs. One side puts up a wall. Well -- well why does a

nation have tariffs? Come on, answer your own
question.

S: Well, I don't understand what a wall is.

T: I'm asking you a very simple question.

*

In this case, the student does not understand the metaphorical use of
the term 'wall'. And since the teacher's discussion did not give any
meaning to this term, the student is left in doubt as to the meaning
of the expression 'tariff wall'.

A more complex form of verbal equivalence definition is that
in which an expression is said to be equivalent to the expression
whose meaning is to be indicated. The following episode from a
history class illustrates this sort of definition.[1]

*

Episode 8   S: It says in the book that the United States was
the sovereign power in the Western hemisphere.
What does that mean?

T: It means they are the strongest ruling power in
the Western hemisphere.

*

The expression 'the sovereign power in the Western hemisphere' means
the same as the expression 'the strongest ruling power in the Western
hemisphere'. In a definition of this type, the meaning of one expression is the same as that of the other expression.

There are at least two symbolic equivalences which are
similar to the verbal equivalence definition. They are abbreviations,
and symbols which are used to stand for values and objects in science
and mathematics. While the rules which apply to the formulation and
use of verbal equivalence definitions appear to hold for these symbolic
equivalences, certain differences should be noted.

Let us consider first the case of an abbreviation. In a

---

[1] In this episode the entry is underlined. This practice will be followed
throughout the report whenever the initial utterance of an episode
contains sentences beside the entry or if there should be any other
reason for doubt as to the location of the entry. In a few cases
there will be two entries.

social studies class a student does not know what the expression 'U.N.' stands for.

*

Episode 9   S: What does 'U.N.' stand for?

                T: United Nations.

*

In this case, the expression 'United Nations' is not a synonym for 'U.N.'. On the contrary, 'U.N.' is a shorthand way of expressing the term 'United Nations'. It is what we ordinarily call an abbreviation.

Let us now consider a symbol which is used to represent a variable in a scientific formula. The teacher is dealing with the subject of velocity in physics. In the class discussion the following episode occurs.

*

Episode 10   T: V_0 has what meaning?

                S: Has the ...

                T: V_0. Now a good way perhaps to remember that
                    is to think of it in this light. Now, we were
                    talking about the sphere rolling across the
                    surface; I said the initial velocity is 100 cms.
                    per second, and then there is a period of time
                    here in which an unbalanced force acts upon the
                    body. And the velocity will change, and the
                    beginning of the time is 0 time. You are just
                    beginning to measure time there. Well, the
                    time involved at the instant you start measuring
                    is 0. So, the sub zero is used to indicate the
                    velocity at that time. We call that V what kind
                    of velocity?

                S: The initial.

                T: The initial velocity.

*

Now in this case, the term 'initial velocity' is not a synonym for the symbol 'V_0'. It is true that as the teacher sets forth the meaning of 'V_0' he at the same time attempts to delineate the meaning of the term 'initial velocity'. And, it is quite clear that 'V_0' is used to refer to the same thing that the term 'initial velocity' represents. But as a symbol in a formula having to do with problems of velocity and acceleration, the symbol $'V_0'$ can have many values. This fact distinguishes this form of symbolic equivalence from strict verbal equivalence definitions.

3. Proper Name Definition

Definitions of this type are given in an effort to answer questions about the meaning of names having a unique referent. For example, in class discussion a teacher or pupil may ask such questions as the following: Who were the Rough Riders? Who was Harrison? Who were the Mohammedans? There was one and only one group of men called the Rough Riders; one and only one man named Harrison who was president of the United States at a particular time, and so on.

Model of Proper Name Definition

Proper
Name ─────────────────────────────⟩ Expression which
identifies the object
referred to by the
proper name

The rules governing the appraisal of proper name definitions may be stated as follows:

a. The expression in the defining part of the definition must uniquely describe the person, place, etc., referred to.

b. The person, place, etc., described in the defining part must be that which the proper name is ordinarily used to refer to, or which authorities agree is the referent of the proper name.

The following episodes illustrate this type of definition.

*

Episode 11   T: Who are the Magi?

S: The Wise Men.

T: The Wise Men, and they took their journey to Bethlehem at Christ's birth. Isn't that right?

*

There was one and only one set of Wise Men who journeyed to Bethlehem

at the time of Christ's birth, and these Wise Men were called the Magi.
This would be considered a unique description of the persons referred
to by the term 'Magi'.

In a history class, the following episode occurs.

*

Episode 12   T: What was the Maine?

                   S: It was just a battleship, and it went over
to Cuba on a friendly mission; it was --
they believed it was sabotaged by some
Spaniards. It blew up and killed two officers
and about 250 men.

                   T: Okay.

*

While the account given by the student does not uniquely describe the
battleship, Maine, in the context of the classroom discourse it does
indicate rather clearly the object for which the word 'Maine' is
used to stand.

Sometimes the definition of a proper name serves a very
limited purpose and holds for a very limited context. In the discussion of a novel in an English class, the teacher wishes to focus
attention on a particular aspect of a story. In doing so, the following episode occurrs.

*

Episode 13   T: What is Sharptown? It isn't so important, but
it is a detail that you should have picked up.

                   S: It is the business district, isn't it?

                   T: Well, a neighboring town, I think.

                   S: Where all the lower -- the one where the poor
people live.

                   T: That's right.

*

The term 'Sharptown' has definite meaning within the story. It is
easy to see that while the expression is not defined in any detail,
its referent is nevertheless identified unmistakably. In the context
of class discussion, 'Sharptown' is defined in such a way as to
constitute a unique description. In the story it is the one and only
neighboring town where the poor people live.

4. Classificatory Definitions

In this type of definition the defining part consists of two elements. The first element is a class term or genus, and the second is the differentia which consists of words referring to the characteristics which distinguish the instances covered by the term being defined from other instances belonging to the genus named by the class term.

Model of Classificatory Definition

Term to be defined ————————————————————→ Class term
(Definiendum)   +
                                            Differentia

The rules for appraisal of classificatory definitions are as follows:
a. The defining part should not contain the term to be defined.
b. The differentia should give enough and no more information than is needed to identify instances to be covered by the term being defined.
c. The definition should be acceptable to authorities in the field represented by the definition.

The differentia may be made up of qualities, functions, processes, and so on, and the class term is of course always an abastraction and never the name of a particular.

Here are some episodes illustrating classificatory definitions.

*

Episode 14   T: What is a dendron?

                     S: The nerve fiber which carries the nerve impulses to the neurons.

                     T: Carries nerve impulses to the neurons.

*

The genus or class term is 'nerve fiber'. The differentia consist in a function or process -- carrying impulses -- rather than in qualities, attributes, or purposes.

But a number of episodes involving definitions could be found in which properties or attributes were indicated as defining characteristics. Here are two examples.

*

Episode 15   T: What is the midbrain?

                  S: The smallest portion of the human brain.

                  T: All right, it's the smallest part.

*

This definition does not give adequate criteria for identifying the midbrain, because the referent of the word 'portion' is vague. If it is understood in the context of class discussion that the brain is divided into three parts, the student's definition is probably adequate for class discussion. At any rate, the episode does illustrate the use of qualities as defining characteristics. The class term or genus in this definition is 'portion of the human brain'. The differentia consists in the expression 'smallest'. It is its size that distinguishes the midbrain from other parts of the brain in this definition.

The other example is as follows.

*

Episode 16   T: What is a rhombus?

                  S: It's a parallelogram with opposite sides equal.

                T: With the opposite sides equal. And one angle is 60° (referring to a particular rhombus drawn on the board), so if these are the smaller angles, here is the 60°.

*

In this illustration, the parallelogram is the genus or class term and the expression 'opposite sides equal', is the differentia or criterion by which a rhombus is distinguished from other parallelograms. While this differentia is inadequate -- the parallelogram must also have oblique angles -- the context of class discussion implies the more adequate statement of differentia.

In some cases, two or more alternative differentia are given as criteria by which to identify instances to be covered by the term to be defined. Definitions of this sort represent a subclass of the

classificatory form. They are usually referred to as disjunctive
definitions. While they occur infrequently in our sample of episodes,
it is of interest to note their structure.

During a physiology class the following episode occurs.

*

Episode 17   T: What is sensory aphasia?

              S: Well, sensory aphasia is that you -- well, the
sight -- you wouldn't be able to receive
impulses, but you'd be able to send them.
Like you wouldn't be able to hear but you
would be able to talk.

              T: All right. It is a condition of those who
cannot understand written or spoken words yet
they can see and hear perfectly well.

*

The differentiae are, first, the inability to understand what is
written, and secondly, the inability to understand spoken words. Now
according to this definition, it would be aphasia if the individual
is unable to understand what is written, even though he can see it,
or it would be aphasia if he were unable to understand what is spoken,
even though he could hear it perfectly well. By either one of these
criteria, it could be said that an individual was suffering from
aphasia.

Teachers employ a number of variations of the classificatory
definition. One of the commonest of these variations is that in which
the class term is omitted and the differentiae alone are given. This
variation is illustrated in the following episode.

*

Episode 18   T: What is a literary snob?

              S: Oh, she thinks she knows it all.

              T: All right. She thinks she knows so much -- that's
elegant and beautiful and fine and artistic, and
she likes to give this impression. She is a
name-dropper. She likes to dress in the latest
clothes, and she's well-read, etc., and people
don't like this very well, do they?

*

It is easy to see that a number of differentiae are given and that the
class term is omitted. The class term in this case is 'snob'. In

other words, a literary snob is a type of snob characterized by certain attributes mentioned in the closing utterance of the teacher.

Here is another example.

*

Episode 19   T: What is an axon?

              S: It carries impulses away from nerve cells or from the neurons.

              T: It carries impulses away from the neurons.

*

Again we see that the student fails to indicate the class of things to which an axon belongs. It belongs to the class of things called 'nerve fibers or parts of a nerve cell', but this fact is not pointed out by the student. Instead, he merely tells us what an axon does; namely, it carries impulses away from nerve cells.

Another variation is a definition in which a statement of the genus or classificatory term alone is given without any differentiae or distinguishing characteristics. An example is as follows.

*

Episode 20   T: How would you define friction?

              S: Resistance.

              T: Friction is a -- what would you say?

              S: Resistance between two bodies.

              T: What do you mean by resistance? Are you talking about electrical resistance? Force is what?

              S: Force is a ...

              T: Oh, excuse me, friction is a what that does what? I practically gave you the answer on that one.

              S: Oh, it's a force.

              T: Force. Friction is a force. Now it is important that you understand that friction is a force.

*

What is known from this definition is that friction is a member of a class of things referred to as force, but not what characteristics distinguish friction as a force from other forms of force. In the course of the discussion in this particular class period, certain criteria are suggested for deciding whether or not a given force is a friction or some other type of force. But these criteria do not show up in this particular episode.

5. Relational Definition

In a relational definition there is a statement of a relationship between two or more attributes or properties. There is no class term, and the statement of relationship gives the meaning of the term to be defined.

Model of Relational Definition

Term to
be defined ──────────────────────> Relation (product,
ratio, etc.)

In a physics class, the teacher and students have been discussing the meaning of the terms 'velocity' and 'acceleration'. They have reached a point in the discussion at which the following episode occurs.

*

Episode 21   T: How will we say $V - V_0$ is the rate of change of velocity? To say, "rate," what do you have to do? A rate implies what sort of mathematical operation?

             S: Division.

             T: Division. We're going to have to divide by something. Well, if we're talking about velocity, and distance, and acceleration and this, and that, and the other, connected with motion -- what do you suppose you divide by?

             S: Time.

             T: Time. So our definition in the form of symbols then would be stated like this. Now, you look at it as it is read. "Acceleration is the rate of change of velocity." Isn't that exactly what that set of symbols says? Here is the change in velocity -- $V - V_0$ divided by the time in which that change occurs. Suppose, going back to our original illustration here -- the ball rolls across the table at an initial velocity of 100 centimeters per second. A force acts upon it which causes it to heat up, and then the final velocity is 210 centimeters per second. Now, there is a difference in the velocity there -- a change in velocity, and an increase in velocity, if you wish -- in this particular case -- of 110 centimeters per second. Now, suppose all of that increase in this particular

case, occurs in 5 seconds. What would be the
acceleration of this object during the time in
which it speeds up? Well -- this would be
acceleration -- will it be equal to 110
centimeters per second? That's the change in
velocity, divided by the time, 5 seconds.

S: It would be equal to ...

T: Talk louder.

S: 70 centimeters per second.

*

Here the teacher defines acceleration as a ratio between $V - V_o$ and t.

Relational definitions are typically used in mathematics and
in the quantitative sciences such as chemistry and physics. They are
found rather infrequently in the social sciences and other content
fields.

6. Definition Entries: Words and Things

An analysis of episodic material indicates that teachers ask
definition questions in many different ways. These ways of asking
such questions may be reduced to two general types. First, the
teacher may form the definition question in such a way as to focus
attention upon a word -- its meaning or its definition. For example,
he may ask: 'What does the word 'pons' mean?' or 'What is the definition of the term 'felony'?'. Second, he may ask the definition
question in such a way as to focus student attention upon what the
word supposedly is used to stand for, rather than upon the word itself.
For example, he may ask: 'What is the midbrain?', 'What is sentiment',
or 'Who are the Magi?'.

Now it would be interesting to know whether or not these
two ways of formulating definition questions call up different types
of reactions. From a logical standpoint, these two ways of putting
a definition question require quite different considerations. When
the question asks for the meaning of a word or for the definition of
a word, it is quite clear that we are asked to talk about the uses of
words. The subject of discussion is a particular word, and we know
that we are expected to tell how the word is used. But when the
definition question asks 'What is an X', the question is ambiguous.

We do not know whether we are asked to give the definition of X or to describe X. The proper reply to the question would be: Do you want a definition or a description?

This distinction cuts deep into the relation of language to objects. It is well-known from psychological investigations that at an early age children tend to identify words and things. This fact is well documented in the work of Vygotsky[2] and in the more extensive studies of Piaget.[3] To change the name of an object is to change its characteristic features. To a child the word 'cow', for example, is attached to a particular object and is so definitely associated with it that the object cannot be called by another name. This claim, of course, will not hold for more mature individuals. Any mature person will readily say that a word is not the same as the thing for which it stands. Yet we find over and over again the tendency on the part of individuals, even those who are highly educated, to assume that if there is a word there must be something -- object, process, whatnot -- corresponding to it. All the sciences have fought to free themselves of this tendency to identify words and things. For example, psychology has fought to rid itself of the idea that because there is a word there is a thing; that there is something corresponding to the word 'mind', to the word 'faculty', and the like.

Now it would seem that the formulation of definition questions in such a way as to ask at one time the meaning of a word and at another time for a description of something for which the word is assumed to stand, represents a confusion of words and things. It is quite clear from episodic material that teachers ask definition questions as though they were dealing with matters of fact. This is the case whenever the teacher asks 'What is so-and-so?'. Let us consider the following example. In a biology class, the subject of the nervous system is being explored. The teacher has turned to a consideration of various aspects of the nervous system, and he has

_____

[2] Vyotsky, L. S. Thought and Language. New York: John Wiley, 1962.

[3] Piaget, Jean. Judgment and Reasoning in the Child. New York: Harcourt, Brace, 1928.

just asked the question of what a neuron is. A student has replied by saying that it carries impulses. The teacher now begins an exploration of the meaning of the term 'impulse'.

*

Episode 22

T: Now, what is an impulse? What <u>is</u> an <u>impulse</u>?

S: It's a stimulation of the sense organs.

T: It's a stimulation of the sense organs. Now what's a sense organ? What would be an example of a sense organ?

S_2: I don't know.

T: (Recognizes a student)

S_3: Touch and see.

T: Touch, sight. What else?

S_4: Smelling.

T: What?

S_4: Smelling

T: Smell.

S_5: Hearing.

T: Hearing, yes. Those would all be sense organs or receptors of certain stimuli. Now, we have not yet defined what an impulse is. We say that these nerves carry impulses. Well, what do they carry? What would it correspond to, or what would it be compared to?

S_6: Electrical -- I don't want to say impulse, but like electrical -- electricity going through wires?

T: All right. It would be much like electricity, yes. It would be moving along this (points to diagram on blackboard) nerve of this neuron, we say, this nerve cell. Some have defined it as a force that is carried by a nerve. Its impulse is set up by some stimulus. We touch the finger; we get a feeling or impression as to whether or not an object is sharp or the shape of it or whether it's hot or cold or wet or dry or -- we get some impression of it. The impulse is set up -- and it's carried to the spinal column, and a response is carried back.

*

The teacher at the very outset formulates his question so as to focus attention upon something called an impulse rather than upon the word 'impulse' itself. In the discussion the students are thinking in terms of a substantive something. This is indicated by the fact that the students immediately turn to sense organs and later to electrical current wires. The teacher also tends to do this when he refers to forces carried by a nerve. At any rate, later on in the episode the teacher restates his question implicitly by saying, "We have not yet defined what an impulse is." He now seems to be asking for the meaning of the term 'impulse', but he very quickly falls back into the descriptive form of the question when he says, "Well, what do they carry? What would it correspond to or what would it be compared to?"

To make the foregoing distinction clear, let us consider an example. A triangle in geometry is defined as a closed plane figure with three and only three sides. Now in the discipline of mathematics, there need not be anything of a material or substantive nature corresponding to the term 'triangle', or for that matter to the term 'plane figure'. In other words, mathematics is a discipline that involves the meaning of symbols without any reference whatsoever to the material world. In this definition of a triangle, it would be pointless to ask whether or not the definition is true in any material sense. The definition is simply a rule for the use of the word 'triangle'. Thus, the rule simply says that wherever the expression 'triangle' occurs in discourse, one can substitute the longer expression 'plane figure with three and only three sides'. Or, wherever the longer expression occurs, he can substitute the shorter one. The meaning is the same in either case, and the question of whether there is anything in reality corresponding to the term 'triangle' or to 'plane figure' or to the expression 'three and only three sides' is irrelevant.

However, it is possible to use the definition in distinguishing among actual figures. That is to say, it is possible to take a large number of figures and to classify them as to whether they are triangles or not. The criteria for so making the classification are laid down in the definition as follows: To be called a triangle, a figure must be a closed rectilinear plane figure and it must have three and only three sides. Any figure which meets these requirements would then be classified as a triangle.

It is clear from this analysis that a definition may be looked at in two senses. First, it may be thought of as merely a rule for using a term, and, second, it may be thought of as a set of criteria for classifying and distinguishing among objects, events, etc., to be covered by the term being defined. In neither case is there any necessary dependence of the defining part of the definition upon the word being defined. Except for conventions of language, it would be possible to substitute any other word for 'triangle' and still keep the defining part of the definition. In other words, the terms and the rules for their use are not dependent upon the particular letters that make up the term nor upon the way in which the term sounds when it is pronounced. The same relationship holds when we look at the second dimension of a definition, namely, to the referent of the defining part of the definition -- the cases to be classified. The term under which these cases are to be classified, that is to say, the term to be defined, could be changed without changing in the least the operation of the defining part of the definition. In short, there is no connection save a conventional one between the term to be defined and the objects, processes, etc., to be classified or covered by the term.

Chapter VII

DESIGNATING EPISODES

To designate is to match words to objects -- persons, events, states, intangibles such as sets and meanings, etc. -- in accordance with conventions of reference, or semantic rules. A designation is the outcome of an act of designating, expressed as a symbol or picture. Designations most often take the form of proper names, common nouns or concise verbal descriptions of objects.

The usual classroom situation in which designating occurs is one in which a designation is the appropriate response to an interrogative stimulus in the entry. Questions containing the interrogatives 'what', 'which', 'who', 'where', and 'when' often require designatory answers. Examples of such questions are: 'What do we call those trees?'; 'What are the different colors of the rainbow?'; 'Which country supported the measure?'; and 'Name the parts of the motor.'. The expectation is usually that the respondent, or designator, will produce a proper designation thereby demonstrating his ability to correctly match names or concise descriptions with the objects under consideration in a lesson. Designations are typically employed in singling out an individual object or set of objects in order to say something about it (i.e., predicate something of it).

1. Analysis of Designating

If designating is viewed as a relation, its domain consists of objects, and its range of designations are usually nouns or nounlike locutions. Its essential logical elements might be diagrammed somewhat as follows:

Object or   _____   Designation
designatum |
                                     |
                                     |
                                     |
                         (Referential) semantic relation
                         of association or matching

Designating differs from referring by being entirely neutral with respect to whether the designatum actually exists. Any nounlike use of a term designates, though there may still be room for disagreement over whether it refers to anything (unicorn, golden mountain, etc.). Much the same could be said about denoting, denotation, etc. Our usage is thus so broad and uncritical as to be in the same class with 'signifying' and 'indicating'. This concept of designating seems to be in accord with an analysis given by Max Black: "Whenever 'E' designates a K, it must be permissible to assert that E is a K, and also to replace 'E' by a 'K' in its original occurrence."[1]

As already indicated designations are made by descriptions as well as by nouns. Designatory descriptions are locutions such as 'the so-and-so' or 'a(n) so-and-so', whose function is to designate rather than to describe. Or rather, such describing as they may do is incidental to their main purpose -- designating. Such descriptions may be definite or indefinite, depending upon whether the definite or indefinite article is appropriate. Thus 'the baldheaded man who lives across the street' is a definite description, since it refers to an individual who is assumed to exist and to be unique.[2] By contrast, 'a man' is an indefinite description, since it designates any of the set of adult male persons. Some such object is assumed to exist, but not to be unique.

We distinguish two main kinds of designating, accordingly as a definite or indefinite designation is appropriate. Instances of picking out a distinct object by the use of a name, noun, or definite description will be called 'identifying', while the use of indefinite designations in giving examples or instances will be called 'specifying'.

2. Types of Designatory Operations

The distinction between identifying and specifying already

---

[1] Black, Max. Models and Metaphors. Ithaca, N.Y.: Cornell University Press, 1962. P. 20.

[2] Bertrand Russell defined a definite description as a set of words purporting to identify a single thing.

mentioned as paralleling the use of the definite and indefinite articles
can be elaborated into a basis for several subcategories within each.
The breakdown we will use is as follows:[3]

      A. Identifying

           1. Associative

               a. Calling

               b. Placing

           2. Selective

               a. Casting

               b. Classing

      B. Specifying

           1. Exampling

           2. Listing

Episodes illustrative of each category above will be presented
in the remainder of this chapter.

3. Identifying Episodes

Associative identifying is distinguished from selective
identifying in that the former demands that an appropriate designation
be recalled or invented by the designator. It might also be called
"constructive" or "operative" identifying to contrast it with selective
identifying, in which the designator chooses from among several alternatives that are available, picking out one from among them as the
correct identification.[4]

The following examples of Calling and Casting may help to
make this clear. The Calling takes place in a physiology class, the
casting in geometry.

---

[3] Terms suggested by John Austin, "How to talk." In J. L. Austin.
Philosophical Papers. (Edited by J. O. Urmson and G. J. Warnock.)
Oxford, England: Oxford University Press, 1961.

[4] The difference between the associative selective forms of identifying
thus strictly parallels that between recall and recognition items in
psychological tests.

*

Episode 1   T: What are the different parts of the brain? Let's begin with the lowest part.

               S: The medulla?

               T: All right.

*

Episode 2   T: The next one, (referring to a diagram on the blackboard) though, how are you going to - or which line are you going to use as the base in number 4? Horizontal, vertical, or an oblique line?

               S: Horizontal.

               T: The horizontal.

*

In the first episode the designation -- 'medulla' -- had to be supplied from memory, where it might have been associated in the student's mind with the description 'lowest part of the brain'. But in the second episode the possible choices were listed and the student expected to select one from among them.

To distinguish now between calling and placing as kinds of associative identifying, compare episode 1 above with the following, also from a physiology class.

*

Episode 3   T: Well what part of the nerve cell is the axon? What structural part?

               S: It's a fiber.

               T: It's a fiber. All right. It carries the impulse away from the nerve cell.

*

Calling, as in episode 1, demands that a name be matched to the object being identified. Placing, as in episode 3, is rather a matter of matching a description to the object.

It is not always easy to tell whether an identification is a name or a description. Semanticists have treated the topic at length, but there seems to be no clear and widely agreed upon distinction. Very roughly, we might say that a name is being demanded when only one identification is acceptable (allowing minor variants of it); but if there might very well be several equally good expressions that bear no

great resemblance to each other as symbols and yet serve to identify
the object unambiguously in each case, these expressions would then be
definite <u>descriptions</u>. But note that this criterion seems to be
violated in episode 3 to the extent that the teacher insists upon
identifying the structural part of the nerve cell as a fiber and
nothing else. In general, however, one would want to characterize a
designation such as 'Kepler' as a <u>name</u> and another such as 'he who
discovered the elliptic shape of the planetary orbits' as a definite
<u>description</u>. Where it is expected that a name will be matched to the
object under consideration we have an instance of calling, e.g., 'what
it is called?'. But if it is instead expected that the object be
"placed" by giving some appropriate characterizing property that serves
to identify it, we might speak instead of placing.

The most common case of calling is that in which the entry
contains a description and a name is to be associated with it. However,
in a few cases a name is used and another (alternative) name is to be
matched to it. Compare episode 1 with the following.

*

Episode 4 T: And <u>do</u> <u>you</u> <u>know</u> <u>what</u> <u>he</u> <u>called</u> <u>the</u> <u>islands</u>?
They weren't Hawaii at that time. Anybody know?
Oh, I think this is an easy name to remember --
especially around noon.

     S: Cook Islands?

     T: No. They weren't Cook Islands. That's a good
guess, but that doesn't happen to be it. The
Sandwich Islands.

     S: Oh.

     T: Do you eat sandwiches at noon, too?

*

Here an alternative name ("Sandwich Islands") has been matched to the
object named in the entry ("Hawaiian Islands"), rather than matching a
name to a described object, as in episode 1. Note that a designatory
term was explicitly asked for in episode 4 -- '... do you know what he
called...?' -- as it necessarily must be in all such name-name
associations. Sometimes names are explicitly asked for in the calling
episodes demanding that a name be associated with a described object
instead of a name.

*

Episode 5   T: Now, what do you mean by the thousand-leggers?
                   What do we call them? What do we call that
                   group scientifically?

              S: Myriapods -- myriapods.

*

In this example from a biology class the group of arthropods described
as 'thousand-leggers' is to be supplied with the proper scientific
name ('What do we call them? ... scientifically?').

The Placing episodes do not exhibit this variation. In all
instances an alternative description is to be fitted to the described
object, as in the following:

*

Episode 6   T: Now, what sets up the impulse to see?
                   What does the light hit in the eye that
                   makes us see?

              S: Retina?

              T: Well, what's in the retina that picks up the
                   stimulus from light?

              S_1: The nerve endings.

              T: The nerve endings in the optic nerve.

*

Here the designatory description 'what the light hits in the eye that
makes us see' is replaced by 'the nerve endings in the optic nerve' in
identifying the object in question. Placing episodes never match
descriptions to named objects; such episodes would be classified in
Describing or perhaps Defining rather than Designating. But the function
of designatory or definite descriptions is to designate, not to describe;
they pick out unambiguously the object about which something else is
being said; saying something about its properties -- describing in the
usual sense -- is incidental and secondary to this purpose. If one
were to "place" Kepler by identifying him as 'the man who discovered
the elliptic shape of the planetary orbits', this would almost surely
have to count as an instance of Describing rather than Designating.

Selective identifying has been contrasted with associative
identifying in that it more nearly resembles a multiple-choice rather
than a fill-in-the-blank situation. Sometimes the items from among

which one is to be selected are explicitly designated, but more often
they are implicit in the situation in which an episode transpires, as
for example, parts of a diagram or words of a sentence on the blackboard. In the above instance of casting -- episode 2 -- the alternatives were quite clearly laid out: horizontal, vertical, and oblique.
For comparison, here is an example from a class in English grammar.

*

Episode 7 T: Well, <u>what</u> <u>is</u> <u>it</u> <u>that's</u> 'clear'? 'Clear' what?

      S: 'Explanation'.

      T: That's what, then?

      S: Because it adds to the adjective 'explanation'.

      T: But 'explanation' isn't an adjective.

      S: It's a noun?

      T: A noun, yes. A noun.

*

From among the words in the sentence under consideration one must be
chosen as the word modified by 'clear'. Only a relatively small
number of possible choices are available from which to select, and it
is quite unnecessary to mention them.

  Episode 7 will serve to illustrate the distinction between
casting and classing as well, since there is in it a quick transition
from the first to the second kind of selective identifying. In the
first part a role or category is stipulated (what it is that's clear,
or the word modified by "clear") and the task is to select the word
that fits it -- i.e., the object that "fills the bill". Something is
to be cast in the role of 'word modified by "clear"' -- an item or
sample must be chosen to fit the pattern. In the second part of
episode 7 the logical situation is inverted. Here an item or sample
is given (the word 'explanation') and the task is instead to match a
role, category, or pattern to it -- in this case, clearly, to class it
as one of the "parts of speech" -- a noun (not an adjective). Casting and classing thus differ as modes of selective identifying in that
the former consists in choosing from among a definite set of objects
one that will fit a given category; the latter, on the other hand,
consists in the inverse operation: choosing from among a definite set

of categories one that will fit a given object.

Classing would not always be easy to distinguish from classifying. The latter term designates operations that may be more complex logically in several ways: e.g., the purpose is not merely to identify an object, but to assign it to the class of things having some further property; more than one object may be given for which a category (or several categories) must be found; the categories may not be predetermined, as is always the case in classing, or relatively few in number, as is usually the case.

To conclude with selective identifying, we note several things about the following examples, from classes in physiology, U.S. history, geometry, and English grammar, respectively.

*

Episode 8 T: Now, here, if you pull out the length of this drawing, you can find fibers out this way. Now, which would be the axon and which would be the dendron?

S: The one on the right would be the axon.

T: The axon. And where would the dendrons be?

S: To the left.

T: To the left. And the entire thing would be the nerve cell or the neuron.

*

Episode 9 T: Bryan carried twenty-two states. Which ones were they?

S: The solid South and the mining areas.

*

Episode 10 T: And, that makes the square root of 225, and that is inches or square inches?

S: Square inches.

*

Episode 11 T: ... then there is a verb which is modified by 'well' which is what?

S: Adverb.

T: Yes. That tells you how he works.

*

Episodes 8 and 9 involve casting; the first offers only two choices, but in the second, one must choose from among all the states those that qualify as ones carried by Bryan in the election under consideration. Episode 8, interestingly enough, remains a two-alternative casting situation whether one considers the choices as 'axon' and 'dendron', or as 'left fiber' and 'right fiber'. Episodes 10 and 11 are instances of classing; the first again presenting just two alternatives -- inches and square inches -- and the second several -- the parts of speech, as one of which 'well' is to be classed.

4. Specifying Episodes

It will be recalled that specifying differs from identifying in that it lacks the force of uniqueness. Existence (in some sense) of an object to be designated is still assumed, but the point here is rather that there are several objects meeting the conditions suggested by the entry, one or more of which are to be designated as specimens or examples of the type under consideration. The task of the specifier is to designate a member or subset of some set that is given or under-stood in the context by mentioning an example, or sometimes to specify all such members or subsets by producing an exhaustive listing. The examples themselves, or items in the list, are instances of identify-ing in that they denote uniquely for the purposes of the matter at hand; presumably it would be inappropriate in most cases to ask for an example within an example (but this is not unthinkable).

'Instance' and 'example' are here used synonymously, although J. L. Austin has suggested a distinction that "when we give examples as opposed to instances we admit a multiformity in the pattern to which justice is not done by one specimen..."[5] The only major distinction to be employed is one of contrasting cases in which one or several from among an indeterminate class of examples are called for with those in which the class is determinate and all examples are to be mentioned.

The following episodes are typical of exampling.

*

Episode 12   T: Now, I have all these pencils -- and give me a comparison.

---

[5] Op. cit., p. 195.

S: The blue one is the largest of the four.

*

Episode 13   T: Another one?

S: Another system is the brain, the nerves, and sense organs.

T: All right.

*

Episode 14   T: Now, will you give me an example of -- several examples of some of our strong hydroxides and also our strong electrolytes. What about some hydroxides?

S: Sodium hydroxide.

T: All right, sodium.

*

These examples, from English, physiology, and chemistry classes, respectively, reveal the three main patterns in exampling: asking for a(n) X (an example of a comparison), another X -- after at least one has been given and can serve as a sample of the kind of thing wanted (another example of a bodily system), or some X's from among the several possible (some examples of hydroxides).

Episodes 15 and 16, from geometry and biology classes, illustrate listing.

*

Episode 15   T: In today's work, we have the three simplest figures -- to measure by square units. <u>What are they</u>?

S: The square, the rectangle, and the triangle.

T: All right.

*

Episode 16   T: Could you name them all?

S: Well -uh- they have -uh- they have a bunch of jaws. They have three jaws -- this is in pairs -- three jaws, I think it meant. They got maxilla -- pair of maxilla -- maxilla, and mandibles two -- and antennae and antennules. Then they've got a bunch of jaws and I never did get that completely straight. And claws and walking legs and swimmerettes. And then the -- well I guess -- the flippers.

T: Flippers. All right, that's pretty good.

*

In these episodes, listing consists in the act of mentioning all the examples in particular categories: something like "simplest rectilinear plane geometric figures" and "gross anatomical parts of a certain marine creature", respectively.   In episode 15 the fact that there are just three examples is given.   In episode 16 there is no suggestion of any definite number needed to constitute a complete list.

5. Summary

To summarize, we list the following brief characterizations of the six types of designatory operations:

    A. Identifying: involves use of the definite article, connoting existence and uniqueness.

        1. Associative: the designation is supplied from memory, or constructed.

            a. Calling: name matched to described or named object.

            b. Placing: description matched to described object.

        2. Selective: designation is chosen from a finite set of evident possibilities.

            a. Casting: select an object to fit a given category.

            b. Classing: select a category to fit a given object.

    B. Specifying: involves use of the indefinite article, connoting existence but not uniqueness.

        1. Exampling: a least one example or instance of a given type is mentioned.

        2. Listing: a complete or exhaustive set of objects or cases of a given type are identified.

Chapter VIII

CLASSIFYING EPISODES

A classifying episode is one in which the student or teacher tells what class or category a given object -- specimen, instance, element, event, etc., -- belongs to, or the general class to which a given type, sort, set, or kind of things belongs as a subclass.

1. Classificatory Behavior

The way a person divides up his world is perhaps one of the most important aspects of his behavior. The divisions or categories into which he places experiences give shape to his cognitive structure as well as to his overt behavior. The individual seldom responds to a particular object or event in itself, but rather responds to it as one of a kind of things. When he responds to it as one of a kind, he does so in anticipation that if certain things are done, certain consequences will follow. He knows that if the object is an apple, it is apt to taste sweet; to make a good pie; to cost so much per dozen, and so on. In other words, as soon as an individual knows that an object is one of a kind of things he responds to the object in terms of its kind -- that is to say, in terms of a body of meanings associated with the class to which it belongs: his apple-concept or apple-image.

Moreover, research often consists primarily in determining the class into which some new phenomenon is to be put. Once the phenomenon is classified, it becomes possible to handle it in terms of the knowledge already existing about the class to which the phenomenon belongs.

It is well to attempt to distinguish classificatory behavior in its complete form from that which we find in the episodic material of the classroom. The logical operation of classifying is much more comprehensive and involved than the behavior found in episodes. To see what the logical operation involves, let us take an example.

Suppose that one were to place before an individual a large number of assorted blocks: blocks of varied colors and shapes and of different heights and weights.[1] Suppose that the individual is asked to classify these blocks. He is not told the categories into which they are to be classified, neither is he told the purpose of the classification, nor given criteria by which the blocks are to be grouped. Instead he is told that he is classify them in any way he chooses for any purpose whatever, and that he must work out the criteria of classification together with the categories.

Now this is the sort of situation which would require the complete logical operation which is referred to here as classifying. In dealing with this situation an individual would have to decide for himself the purpose for which his classificatory scheme is to be used. He would have to decide the criteria by which the blocks are to be classified. His classificatory system should be such that no block is left unclassified, and his criteria should be of such a nature that anyone could take the same criteria and succeed in classifying the blocks the same way.

The student is seldom if ever required to engage in this sort of classificatory operation. We found no evidence in our episodic materials that the student is ever called upon to take a collection of objects and to work out a way of classifying them. Instead, the classificatory behavior called for in the classroom is almost entirely verbal. A student does not see or deal directly with the objects and events which he is asked to classify, except occasionally in such courses as biology and chemistry. His task usually is to recall the class to which the particular instance belongs. If he is asked to tell what class of things a starfish belongs to, usually he simply mentions the class name. Nor is he required ordinarily to give the characteristics of Asterias rubens to which the common starfish belongs. Occasionally, he may have before him an actual instance -- a seashell, a snake, or an insect -- and with the proper guide or

[1] For example, blocks like those used in various psychological experiments in concept-formation. See Eugenia Hanfmann and J. Kasanin. A method for the study of concept formation. J. Psychol., 1937, 3, 521-540.

handbook he is asked to ascertain the class species to which the particular in his possession belongs. In these cases, he is using established classes and official criteria by which to place instances or specimens into proper categories.

The procedure in school is one in which both the teacher and the student work with categories already established. It is the teacher's task to help the student learn predetermined categories and to what particular category a given instance belongs, or to what general class a given subclass belongs. Neither is the student taught the structure of existing categories so as to understand the criteria they entail nor is he made aware that such criteria exist. In other words, the episodic material indicates quite clearly that the student is repeatedly telling the kind of thing something is without ever going into the question of how you tell in any case the kind of thing it is.

It is not the purpose here to evaluate the procedure with which the teachers deal with classification. Rather, the purpose is to describe what is actually done in the classroom with the logical operation of classification. What the teacher does may be an effective mode of teaching. This is an empirical question and can be answered only in the light of further evidence. But it is well before such further investigation is undertaken to know what in fact the teacher ordinarily does in the classroom with classificatory questions.

2. Model of Classifying

Reduced to its skeletal form, the model of the classificatory operation is as follows:

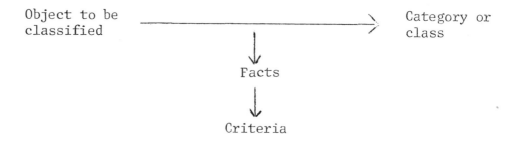

This diagram shows that the operation of classifying involves at least four factors: (a) the object to be classified, (b) the category into which it is to be classified, (c) the criteria by which to decide whether the object belongs in the particular category, and (d) the facts of the case, that is to say, characteristics of the object which in terms of the criteria indicate that the object should be placed in the particular category.

In the classroom situation the teacher and the students work with categories which are already given in the subject matter with which they are dealing. And, as a rule, the students are given only one or two cases to classify at a time, and the decision which must be made is usually one of whether or not the particular case belongs in a category which is either itself given or which must be supplied by the student.

3. Types of Classificatory Operations

In the analysis of episodic material, we have been able to identify six different sorts of classificatory acts. In their complete form each one fits the model above, but practically no episode exhibits all four factors of the model. In short, classificatory behavior in the classroom is elliptical.

Henry Hiz has noted in a recent paper that Aristotle advocated an interrogative methodology of knowledge.[2] Knowledge could be classified, he thought, according to the kind of question to which it provides an answer. Following this lead, we might classify the utterances in various classroom episodes according to the kinds of questions involving classifying to which they are explicitly or implicitly answers.

Suppose that we denote the object to be classified by 'X', letting A be a class of which a is a subclass. Then what transpires in a classifying episode may then be viewed as in effect an attempt to pose or answer such questions as the following:

1. To what class does X belong? (Supply its designation.)
2. To which class of those given does X belong? (Choose one.)

---

[2] Questions and answers. _Journal of Philosophy_, 10 May 1962, 59, 253-265.

3. Does X belong to class A? (Yes or no.)

4. To what subclass of A does X belong? (Again, supply the answer.)

5. To which subclass of those given does X belong? (Choose one.)

6. Does X belong to subclass a of class A? (Yes or no.)

Evidently one kind of operation is called for in 1 and 4, another in 2 and 5, and a third in 3 and 6. Within these operations there are the cases covered in 1, 2, and 3 on the one hand, in which the question might be asked with respect to the class A, and the 4, 5, and 6 cases, on the other, in which a subclass of some given class A is in question. In schematic form the six kinds of classifying would then be:

	Class	Subclass of given class
Supply (construct) the answer	1	4
Choose (pick out) the answer	2	5
Answer yes or no	3	6

When the number of choices is reduced to two, types 3 and 6 collapse into 2 and 5, respectively; psychologically speaking, 2 and 5 might become very much like 1 and 4 when the number of choices offered is rather small. The left and right columns would tend to merge when it was not clear whether the class in question was being considered as a subclass of some other class which subsumes it.

Type 1. X (object to be classified) is given in the entry, and the name of the class to which it belongs is supplied.

The following episodes will illustrate this mode of classification. In an English class, a teacher and the students are discussing a particular character.

*

Episode 1   S: And Yusef is a --

T: Not Catholic.

S: Mohammedan.

T: Mohammedan. Right

*

Episode 2   T: All right, let's get this one straightened
                  first. 'Definitely' ranks as a what? And
                  'very' is what?

             S: That adds to the adverb, doesn't it?

             T: I can't hear you.

             S: It adds to the adverb, doesn't it?

             T: To what adverb?

             S: 'Definitely'.

             T: Yes.

*

It is interesting to note in these two episodes that while the student performs a classificatory operation, he gives no criteria by which to decide that the object being classified belongs in the particular category. For example, in the case of Yusef it is decided that he is a Mohammedan rather than a Catholic. But the criteria by which one decides that an individual is a Mohammedan and not a member of some other religious sect are not given. Nor are we given any factual characteristics of Yusef which might have been implied by a criterion.

In the second episode, the student looks at the sentence and notes that 'very' modifies 'definitely'. He then states the fact that 'very' adds to the adverb 'definitely'. He fails to classify the word 'very', leaving the categorization of the term to implication. It is apparently understood from the fact that 'very' modifies an adverb that 'very' is itself an adverb. Neither the criterion for deciding what class of words 'very' belongs to nor the class itself is stated.

Type 2. X and the classes to which it might belong are both mentioned in the entry, and a decision is to be made as to which of them it is a member.

The following episode from a U. S. history class illustrates this type of operation.

*

Episode 3   T: But I think there's one other thing you've got
                  to keep in mind. Why are we talking about
                  Jackson this way? What do you call Jackson?
                  Is he a conservative? Radical? Reformer?

Carolyn: Radical.

    T: Yes, he comes close to being a radical.

*

Here the possible choices are 'conservative', 'radical', and 'reformer'; the task is then to decide which of them President Andrew Jackson should be called -- in other words, to pick out one of the three as the proper category for Jackson.

*

Episode 4   B: Wouldn't the juvenile delinquent, more or less, be under adventure seeker?

    T: Under what?

    B: The first one -- adventure seeker?

    T: Maybe. Maybe. We have some, perhaps, who are past the juvenile stage.

*

In this episode a list of types of lawbreakers is before the class; one is chosen as the proper classification for juvenile delinquents.

In another class, a book is being discussed from the standpoint of the kind of information it contains.

*

Episode 5   T: Do you think of it as scientific information, or biographical information, or what kind?

    P: Well, scientific. They have usually at the beginning of each chapter about the different scientists -- they have about two or three paragraphs about his life. Then, they go into what he has covered and (teacher interrupts)

    T: Essentially -- okay. Essentially, then it has to do with these ideas in science rather than the men of science -- the background of it. Okay.

*

What is asked for in this episode is a classification of the kind of information which is given in the particular book. The student is given two categories into which to classify the information -- a scientific category and a biographical category -- and, in addition, the teacher leaves the question of categories somewhat open by adding "or what kind". The student classifies the information as being scientific. Even though he recognizes that there is a considerable amount of biographical material, on the whole he judges the information to be scientific. The teacher tries to make this point clear by indicating that the information in the book deals with ideas in science rather than with accounts about men as scientists. It is of interest to note, however, that in this case as in the preceding cases, the criteria by which information is to be classified as scientific, biographical or what, are not stated. They are merely taken for granted, and a judgment made as to the kind of information contained in the book without explicit reference to the criteria as such. The student does note certain facts which might be relevant to an adequate criterion: paragraphs about the lives of scientists followed by treatments of what they did.

Type 3. X and the class to which it might belong are both mentioned in the entry, and a decision is made as to whether X belongs to the suggested class.

This type of operation differs from Type 1 in that the class to which X might conceivably belong is named. In Type 1 no class name is mentioned. The question of what class X belongs to is left open, and the student is required to supply it. In Type 3, however, the class to which X possibly belongs is mentioned, and the student must decide whether or not X belongs to the suggested class.

Here is an episode illustrating this type of classificatory operation. In a biology class, the various systems of the human body are being discussed.

*

Episode 6   S: Would you put that (tympanic membrane) under the nervous system?

           T: Yes.

           S: The integumentary system?

           T: Well, you can put the tympanic membrane, because it is almost on a line with the skin. You could put it under both of them. It really belongs, of course, in the nervous system, but you could put it under integumentary system.

*

Note that the name of the category into which the tympanic membrane may be classified is given. In fact, the student suggests two

categories with the apparent implication that it could be classified
under either one. The teacher confirms the pupil's hunch in this case.
He says the tympanic membrane can be classified under the integumentary
system, and he gives as a reason the fact that it is on a line with the
skin. But we are not told why the tympanic membrane being on a line
with the skin is reason for classifying the membrane under the
integumentary system. Then the teacher goes ahead to say that it can
also be classified under the nervous system, and, in fact, he says
that is where it really belongs. But again, we are given no reason
for this particular claim.

Type 4. X and the class to which X belongs are both named
in the entry, and the name of the subclass to which X belongs is
supplied.

This sort of Classificatory operation requires that an
individual think in terms of subclasses. He knows that the object to
be classified belongs to a particular category which is named, and his
task is to decide what subclass the object belongs to.

The following episodes will illustrate this operation.

*

Episode 7   T: All right now, what kind of people are the
                     Jarvis' and the Harrison's?

                  S: They were wealthy.

                  T: Wealthy what?

                  S: (Inaudible remark)

*

Episode 8   T: Now, when he, indirectly in the beginning
                     mentions Mrs. Scobie and then later he refers
                     to her, what kind of person is Mrs. Scobie,
                     so far?

                  S: She's awfully ambitious.

                  T: She's what?

                  S: Ambitious.

                  T: All right.

                  S: And she's sort of a literary snob.

*

In these two examples we see cases in which a category is mentioned

-- in the first episode, the given category is people and in the second episode, the category is person -- and the student is asked to tell the kind, that is to say, the subclass of people and of persons to which the instances belong. Thus the Jarvis' and the Harrison's belong to the subclass 'wealthy people' and Mrs. Scobie is classified as belonging to the subclass 'ambitious person' or 'literary snob'.

Again, the classificatory act is performed without any criteria being stated or requested, either by the students or the teacher. Furthermore, the factual characteristics by which the Jarvis' and the Harrison's are classified as 'wealthy people' in terms of criteria are not given. The same thing can be said about the classification of Mrs. Scobie as an 'ambitious person' or 'literary snob'.

Type 5. X and the class to which X belongs are both mentioned in the entry together with the subclasses to which X might belong, and a decision is made as to which subclass X does in fact belong.

The following episode illustrates this kind of operation.

*

Episode 9   T: What specific figure of speech would you say
                 this is? Is it a metaphor or a simile? That
                 the voice has magic in it; it has threatening
                 in it; it is as though Africa itself were in it;
                 a lion growls in it: and thunder echoes in it
                 over black mountains.

             G: I think it's a metaphor. Because it doesn't say
                 "like" or "as". Just says "is".

             T: Just in one place -- it says "a lion growls" --

is a metaphor. But when he says "it is as though Africa were in it"--

B: Yeah, that's a simile.

T: That's a simile. O.K.

*

In this episode the background class is designated by 'figures of speech' and the students are requested to choose between the subclasses 'metaphor' and 'simile' as the proper classification of the figures of speech under discussion.

Here some relevant facts are adduced after the "because" in the second utterance, but the generalization justifying the categorization (i.e., the criterion) is left in a kind of enthymematic ellipsis.

Type 6. X and the class to which X belongs are both mentioned in the entry together with the subclass to which X might belong, and a decision is made as to whether X belongs to the suggested subclass or not.

This classificatory act differs from that of Type 4 only in the fact that in Type 4 the subclass must be supplied; it is left unnamed and is hence open-ended. In the present type of operation the student is required to decide whether or not the particular instance belongs in the suggested subclass. He is not required to supply a subclass, but rather is given one and asked to decide whether or not it is appropriate in the particular case. Consider as examples the following episodes which occur in discussing a novel.

*

Episode 10   T: Now he, in a sense, why he -- I'll put it this way, do you think he is the kind of man who misrepresents his thoughts?

S: No, because he's an honest man.

*

Episode 11   T: All right. Now, Scobie is actually talking against truth here. Does this seem typical? Is he the sort of person who sees what nobody else sees in his daily living?

S: No.

*

In the first of these episodes, a particular character in a novel is being discussed. The class -- man -- to which the character belongs is stated. And a subclass of the category is also given -- the kind of man who misrepresents his thoughts. The student is then required to decide whether or not the particular character is a member of this subclass. The student decides that the character does not belong to this subclass and he gives as a reason "he is an honest man." In other words the criterion for belonging to the subclass -- those who misrepresent their thoughts -- is that one must be dishonest. And since the character in this novel is an honest man, he is not a member of the subclass named by the teacher. The same thing can be said of the second episode. The teacher wishes to know whether or not Scobie belongs to the subclass of persons who "see what nobody else sees in his daily living". The student says "no", and gives no reason for his answer.

4. Epistemic Rules for Classification

The following are epistemic rules for classificatory operations:

1. The criteria for grouping the elements of a domain into classes should exhaust all elements in the domain, while not permitting overlap among the classes; in other words, the criteria should define a partition of the domain.

2. The criteria should be clear; that is to say, their application should be evident and observable.

3. The criteria should be dependable. What they purport to be the case should have a high degree of probability of being the case. Ideally, a criterion should be based on this sort of relationship: attribute q is characteristic of elements of kind p. That is to say, that the following statement should be true: Whatever has attribute p also has the attribute q. This statement should be true either by definition or as a matter of empirical fact. Where the sentence is not true in every case, the probability

of its being true should be fairly high.

4. In a scientific field, the criteria should be acceptable
   to the authorities of the particular field. Where criteria
   have not been established, they should satisfy as nearly as
   possible rules 1 through 3 above.

Some discussion of these rules together with a brief explanation of the kinds of contexts in which they are used would seem to be
in order.

In domains where there is a well developed classificatory
system, as in biology, chemistry, and geometry, the classification of
instances as belonging to this or that class is said to be correct if
they satisfy the "official" criteria. If an animal is classified as
a vertebrate, we know that the classification is correct provided the
particular animal has a backbone composed of either bone or cartilage.
The criterion that must be met in order that a specimen be a vertebrate
is: the presence of a backbone. If the animal does not have a backbone, we know that the classification is incorrect. In mathematics
we know that if a plane figure is classified as a triangle, the
classification is correct provided the figure has three and only three
sides. In such cases, there are accepted criteria by which to decide
whether or not a given object belongs in the particular class. And
any act of classification is considered correct if it meets the
accepted criteria.

There are many domains, however, in which there are no widely
accepted criteria for deciding whether or not an object belongs in a
particular category. A few questions taken from episodic material will
illustrate some of these domains. What kind of home does he live in?
What kind of column does he write? What kind of people were they? Now
people live in all sorts of homes and they write all sorts of columns
and, of course, there are all sorts of people. But the criteria by
which to decide whether an instance of such domains belongs to a
particular sort or kind are not established. An individual may live
in a shanty, or in a mansion, or in some sort of a home between these
two extremes. But the criteria for deciding whether or not a house is
a shanty or a mansion have no such "official" status as do the criteria

in a scientific or mathematical system. Some individuals might classify a house as being a shanty if it is unpainted and located in a particular part of a community. Other persons may classify a house as a shanty on the basis of what it costs. And still others may use as a criterion that the house simply looks shabby. Some variation in criteria is found in all imprecise terminology and concepts.

For certain purposes, it sometimes becomes necessary to set up standards for making judgments about the appropriateness or inappropriateness of the member of a given domain for which precise criteria have not been established. For example, the Federal Housing Administration has had to establish for its operation certain criteria by which to judge the adequacy of houses. Also, if one were making a study of housing, he would be required to have some set of criteria by which to decide the houses which are adequate and those which are in-adequate. In such cases, the criteria may concern such characteristics as the age, the degree of crowding, the state of repairs, the plumbing, and the equipment in houses. These, of course, are not criteria but they are aspects of houses about which criteria might be formulated.

In cases of this sort, the question of the validity of the classificatory act which students engage in is not easy to settle. As a matter of fact, if one student says that a house is such-and-such a kind and another student disagrees, the teacher is often at a loss to know how to settle such a difference of opinion. There is no accepted set of criteria to which he can appeal, and he is apt to treat the matter merely as one of opinion. This is ordinarily the case in literature and the social sciences, and, in fact, in most of the school subjects which do not belong to the so-called natural sciences or to mathematics.

Thus far we have been talking about the status of criteria used in the act of classifying. It has been noted that in some domains there are not generally accepted criteria, but rather the criteria are either grounded in some small reference group or else in individual preferences.

In addition to status, one other consideration should be noted. The criteria used in classifying may be vague to the point that it is difficult to employ them. Or, they may be extremely clear and concise. For example, if we wish to classify individuals as to whether they belong in the class of genius or not, the criterion might be: anyone who has an intelligence quotient of 180 or above will be called a genius; and anyone who has an intelligence quotient less than 180 will not. In this case, the criterion is completely clear even though it may not be accepted by everyone, or even by everyone in the smaller reference group called psychologists and educators. According to the criterion, there would be two groups of people. Those who qualify as geniuses and those who do not. There can be no overlapping, for by the criterion it is possible to classify all individuals into these two groups. By a criterion of this sort it is possible to create a category system which is both exhaustive and exclusive. The same thing can be said about classification in any domain where the criterion is strictly logical in the sense that the categories are determined purely by stipulation.

There are cases, however, where the criteria are so vague that it is impossible to tell whether or not a particular instance satisfies them. For example, suppose we wish to classify a number of cups according to colors and color values. We might then have a category of cups called "blue" with a subclass of categories called "light blue", "dark blue", etc. Now the criteria which might be specified for a light blue subclass could be so vague that it will be most unlikely that one would classify the cups in the same way anyone else would classify them by the same criterion. Even were we to specify as a criterion that light blue will be the color which falls between this particular specified color -- a sample being given -- and this particular specified color -- a sample being given -- it would still be vague. For there would be some cups that would be so near the border at either extreme that one would not know into what subclass of color values they should be put. Criteria of this nature show up over and over again in our episodic material.

Finally, there is the question of the reliability of the criterion itself. A criterion may be clear and generally accepted and yet not be dependable in every case. For example, at a commonsense level, it is ordinarily considered that an individual has a headache if he continues to frown and to hold his head. He is classified by this criterion as being an individual who belongs to the class of persons who at the moment have a headache. Now it so happens that people hold their heads and frown for many different reasons, only one of which is because of an aching head. So, if the criterion used for classifying people into two categories -- those who have headaches and those who do not -- is that they hold their heads and frown, we could not be certain in a particular case that we had correctly classified an individual. A criterion of this sort is a probabilistic one, and, its reliability may range from near zero to nearly perfect dependability.

Criteria of this sort are usually grounded in matters of fact rather than in definitions, as in the case of the categories in mathematics. These criteria are usually related to the classificatory scheme by empirical regularities or by correlations which have varied orders of dependability.

In our episodic material there are a number of classificatory operations which are based upon criteria of a formal, definitional character. These are found largely in the field of grammar and mathematics. In the case of parts of speech for example, words are classified according to certain grammatical rules. These rules hold without exception. For example, a word may be classified as an adverb by the following criterion: an adverb modifies a verb, or an adjective, or another adverb by expressing time, place, manner, degree, etc.

In other cases, our episodic materials are concerned with empirical criteria of various sorts. Thus, for example, chemical equations may be classified as either exothermic or endothermic, and the criterion in these cases is an empirical one. Likewise in physics, there are many empirical criteria for classifying phenomena. In the social sciences and humanities the criteria are often empirical, and are either vague or so lacking in dependability that it is often difficult to apply them decisively.

5. Alternative Modes of Classification

At least two other ways of grouping Classifying episodes were considered. It would have been relatively easy to classify the episodic material into content categories. The episodes would then have been classified into such categories as mathematics, social studies, English, and so on. While this mode of classification would have been useful for certain purposes, it was discarded because it probably would have had little or no logical significance. The logical structure of the classificatory operation does not depend upon the nature of the content. Nor do the criteria which are used in the classification of elements of a domain into various classes depend upon the content in such a way as to render this mode of classification useful for our purposes.

A second mode of classification is one which would have been based upon certain logical considerations. We could have grouped classifying episodes into certain categories, depending upon the way classificatory criteria are themselves formulated. We could have had a category of analytic classificatory episodes. This class of episodes would have been one whose criteria are determined simply by definition. For example, as we saw above, the class of plane figures called "triangles" is determined purely by definition. We could have had a second set of episodes called empirical. Episodes of this type would have been classified by empirical relations between the attributes of the instances and the category into which the particular element was placed. This sort of classificatory scheme would have included most of the empirical sciences.

Then we could have had an additional category called quantitative. We have reference here to such classes as hot and cold, wet and dry, hard and soft, etc. These are quantitative categories in that there is a wide variation in the amount of the attributes by which any given object is classified into categories of this type. An object would be classified either as cold or hot if its temperature falls within a range of temperatures. Or, the classification of objects into hard objects and soft objects would again entail some way of ordering objects in terms of hardness or softness. This, of course, could be done by the relation of scratches. That is to say, one object would be said to be harder than another if it scratches the other and is not scratched by it. In this way the categories of hardness could be established but they would be based upon relative empirical relations.

This mode of classification, while significant logically, was not used for the simple reason that it did not seem as pedagogically relevant as the way in which we actually did classify the episodes. The actual classification worked out above is more closely related to the way in which teachers handle the subject matter in the classroom than are these two alternative ways of grouping classificatory episodes.

Chapter IX

COMPARING-CONTRASTING EPISODES

The term 'compare' is often used to refer to statements of
differences as well as resemblances between two or more items -- actions,
events, concepts, concrete objects, etc. For this reason, the title of
the category is hyphenated, and the two speech-acts of comparing and
contrasting are considered within a single category. Just as items
to be compared must possess some features in common, so too, only
items that are heterogeneous in at least one respect can be contrasted.
While comparison and contrast can be made among several items our
sample of episodes present only two items of the same general type,
except in the case of analogy.

Comparing-contrasting rests upon several other major categories, e.g., describing and evaluating, which function in episodes
as substrata upon which the category of comparing-contrasting is
superimposed. Two items are described, for example, and on the basis
of this description found either to be alike or to differ. Consider
the following episode from a biology class:

*

Episode 1   T: Now how do they differ, though? Compared
                       to that in the grasshopper, or compared to
                       that in the fish?

                   S: Fish's eye is not compound.

                   T: That's it. That's what we want. It's
                       not compound.

*

The entry merely notes that a difference does exist between the items
in question. The response describes one item of the pair, and thereby
indicates the difference between them.

1. Episodes Involving a Given Standard

The first subcategory of comparing-contrasting episodes may
be described as one in which a basis or standard for the comparison or

contrast is given in the episode. Usually this basis is explicitly
mentioned in the entry of the episode.

Frequently only a single standard is given. The entry gives
two elements: the objects to be compared or contrasted and the
standard by which they are to be compared or the basis on which comparison is to be made. In the entry of an episode taken from a
biology class, the basis -- size of the grasshopper's eye -- is
immediately set up.

*

Episode 2   T: Was his eye very large compared to the
size of the grasshopper?

                    S: Nope.

                    T: Oh, you think the eyes are small.

                    S: Grasshoppers' eyes are small.

                    T: Ah -- the grasshopper's eye is small.

*

'His eye' and that of the grasshopper are the items to be compared;
size is the basis of the comparison and serves to direct the operation
of comparing. In other words, the two kinds of eyes are not simply to
be compared or contrasted, but they are to be compared on the basis of
a single feature -- size.

Episodes in which more than one standard or basis for comparison is given have the same general pattern as those in which only
a single standard is provided.

The following episode, taken from a history class, expressly
sets up three bases on which to compare or differentiate Japan and
China at a given historical period.

*

Episode 3   T: China was a tremendously large country.
But was it a very powerful country from
the standpoint of wealth, and literate
population, a well organized army, and
all those other things? Had it really been
a very good match for the Japanese army as
they had --- in this period? What do you
think about that?

                    S: The Chinese weren't any match for the Japanese
Army -- didn't have a very large standing army,

> had a lot of people; most of them weren't
> in it, so probably it was a very easy fight.

> T: Most of them were very poor peasant groups.
> But you did have wealth in the cities; they
> didn't have the Emperor with very great
> control over them.

*

These three factors -- wealth, literate population, and well-organized
army -- are more than bases of comparison; more accurately, they are
mentioned as standards against which the two cultures are to be comparatively measured. The act of comparing is directed to these
standards. The responses to the entry express the belief that the
two cultures are not very similar with respect to the given standards.

2. Episodes In Which No Standard Is Given

In most comparing-contrasting episodes no basis for comparing the two items is given. Instead the entry presents the items and
then requires that they be compared or contrasted in a general way.
The student is free to select a basis on which to develop the comparison.

In a biology episode the entry asks that the frog heart be
differentiated from the fish heart.

*

Episode 4　　　T: What about their heart? How did that
　　　　　　　　　 differ from the fish that we talked about?

　　　　　　　　 S: In the frog, there are three chambers and
　　　　　　　　　 while in the fish, there aren't.

　　　　　　　　 T: How many do we have in the fish?

　　　　　　　　 S: The heart's just one -- two chambers: auricle
　　　　　　　　　 and ventricle.

*

The entry merely asks how the two kinds of hearts differ, no basis
being given for making the ensuing contrast.

Similarly, the following episode from a chemistry class asks
that a difference be noted between two items, but does not mention any
respect in which the items may be found to differ.

*

Episode 5   T: What <u>is the difference</u> between <u>organic and
                      inorganic</u>? He talks about organic compounds,
                      and he talks about inorganic and what is the
                      difference or what -- give me an example.

                   S: Would inorganic be those which are acids and
                      bases and things like that, and organic be
                      the ones that are derived from animals,
                      fossils, and things like that?

                   T: Well, most of the -- as far as <u>most</u> of the
                      organic compounds have what in <u>them</u>? Carbon --

                   S: Carbohydrates.

                   S_1: Carbon and hydrogen.

                   S_2: Carbohydrates.

*

The response differentiates the items with respect to a very general,
almost ambiguous chemical classification. This classification is then
narrowed down to specific chemical content.

3. Episodes Which Give Comparisons

Clearly different from the first two forms of comparing-contrasting, this subcategory gives only one item together with the basis
of the comparison, or else, the comparison itself, and then asks that
the comparable or contrasting item be located. In the other subcategories, both items of the comparison have been provided in the
entry, and they were then compared with regard to one or more bases
either specified or decided by the student. But in the subcategory
now being considered only one pole of the comparison is given.

    In the following example from a biology class, only one
item of the comparison is provided; the act of comparing consists in
finding the other.

*

Episode 6   T: What's the opposite of the word "dorsal"
                      -- that we have?

                   S: The ventral side?

                   T: The ventral side.

*

The relationship between the two items is specified by the term
'opposite', as being so opposed in meaning that each contradicts. But
the items are not themselves described in order to point out how they
indeed compare or differ. Rather, only one side of the relation is
given; and the comparison is then made simply by supplying the other
pole of the relation.

   An example taken from an English class, discussing a
metaphor used in a novel, provides one item in a relationship -- a
man sleeping in the grass -- describes its relation to the missing
item as one of comparison, and then requires that the missing item be
supplied.

*

Episode 7   T: And then Kumalo says -- and here is one of
                 the very beautiful metaphors in this book,
                 "'There is a man sleeping in the grass....
                 and over him is gathering the greatest storm
                 of all his days. Such lightning and thunder
                 will come there as have never been seen before,
                 bringing death and destruction. People hurry
                 home past him, to places safe from danger.
                 And whether they do not see him there in the
                 grass, or whether they fear to halt even a
                 moment, but they do not wake him they let
                 him be.'" (Stops reading and addresses class)
                 Now, what is he comparing this man to? What's
                 this good man lying in the grass with a storm
                 coming over him make you think?

             S: Is it supposed to be himself?

             T: It's supposed to be himself? Well, now that
                 would be the literal meaning of it, wouldn't it?
                 But what does it mean? What does it represent?
                 What is it symbolizing? What is the metaphor?

           S_1: Well -- it's to show how the people of the
                 town....

             T: Now, you're being literal minded again. You're
                 telling us the story -- you're not telling us
                 the symbolism. You're not giving us the
                 metaphor.

           S_2: /Inaudible remark/

             T: Well, we've already said that. That's being
                 literal minded. What's -- what's behind it?

           S_3: Well, a man can /inaudible 1 second/ and it
                 isn't fair and people see him and /inaudible
                 2 seconds/ but half of them would never tell
                 him until they happen to see a storm in his

face and --

T: Who is the man?   /Students mumble/
You're literal minded!   /Students mumble/
What is the metaphor here? Who is the man!

S₄: The people of South Africa.

T: The people of South Africa! The country is
sleeping in the grass.

*

The act of comparing, thus, consists in finding the unknown, comparable
item -- the people of South Africa. The force of the metaphor is found
in the sensitivity of the people to the sleeping man.

Chapter X

CONDITIONAL INFERRING EPISODES

The conditional inference episode is one in which certain conditions are given and an individual must decide what will be the case, or what he will do, were these conditions to obtain. Besides giving the conditions, the entry indicates what the questioner is interested in knowing, although episodes exhibit varying degrees of specificity in this regard. Usually the teacher, or the student if he initiates the episode, is not interested in everything that would be the case or that the individual would do under the given circumstances. He wishes to know only a particular consequence of the specified conditions.

1. Problems of Analysis

The entries of conditional inferring episodes take a variety of forms. Words such as 'if' and 'when' are reliable indicators of such episodes, and the entries of a large proportion of these episodes include one or the other of these clues, usually as stems. For example, 'If you tried to stop thinking, could you?' and 'What's the altitude when the angle is 30°?' are entries which are readily recognizable as requiring conditional inferences. There are other entries, however, which are not so easily classified. Consider the following: 'Consequently, instead of trying to count them (square units in an area) what do we do about it?' and 'What did you do with it after you had used it -- 1.414?'. While these entries are not cast in terms usually associated with conditional statements, they do express conditions. One part of these entries qualifies or limits the context in which the question is to be considered, e.g., 'after you've used it' limits the context in which the question 'What did you do with it?' is to be considered.

The diversity in the form and content of entries together with vagaries and ambiguities in the body of the episode renders it difficult to make logically significant distinctions among conditional inferring episodes. Obviously such episodes can be analyzed in a number of ways. For one thing, they can be analyzed into the types of conditions given in the entry. These conditions may consist of empirical material such as descriptions of events or states of affairs. They may be either historical or hypothetical. Or they may be made up primarily of conventional or prescribed materials such as grammatical rules and mathematical definitions and axioms. While this mode of analysis may have certain advantages for pedagogical purposes, it nevertheless obscures the logical distinctions involved in teaching operations.

Another mode of analysis is that of sorting out the episodes in accordance with the amount of freedom the specified conditions allow for inference. Classification of episodes in this way would, of course, result in a continuum, one end of it representing episodes in which there is no freedom of inference and the other end episodes allowing complete freedom. Where the conditions constitute the premises and the consequent the conclusion of a deductive argument, the individual would have no freedom of inference since there is one and only one correct inference which can be made. Suppose a teacher says 'If you are given the numbers 2, 9, 16, 23, what will the next number be?'. It is clear that the teacher is expecting as an answer a particular number. This entry shapes a closed situation in the sense that it makes one and only one correct answer possible. At the other end of the continuum would be episodes which were completely open. For example, suppose the teacher says 'If man had had no thumb, what would have been the course of civilization?'. This entry exhibits little specificity with respect to answers which the teacher might anticipate and the situation is hence an open one. Only in a general sense can it be said that the entry indicates what the teacher is interested in knowing. Most conditional inferring episodes fall between these two extremes.

Episodes which maximize freedom of inference are of particular significance today, for they are emphasized in the so-called discovery method of teaching. This method specifies a set of conditions to which the student is supposed to respond in a novel fashion. In some cases his creativity is judged to be in direct proportion to the number and variety of unusual responses he can make to the given conditions.

For the purposes of the current project, the chief objection to this mode of analyzing conditional inference episodes is that it is primarily psychological. It involves no significant logical distinctions and consists primarily in applying a psychological criterion -- the amount of inference freedom.

One is always tempted to take the easy way out in analyzing episodes. One of the easy ways is to classify episodes by content as, for example, in the school curriculum. Accordingly, one would classify conditional inferences into categories based upon mathematical, historical and biological content, and so on. However, this mode of classification is not likely to involve significant logical distinctions, since in many cases the logical character of a conditional inferring episode in history, for example, would differ in no significant way from the logic of such an episode in biology, chemistry, or English. Furthermore, there would probably be several logically distinct kinds of episodes within history, several within biology, etc.

It is possible to group Conditional Inference episodes in terms of the sort of justification their inferences require. To take some examples: in inferences such as those made in grammar, the justification would consist in a rule of grammar or definition or both; inferences in geometry would be justified in terms of definitions and postulates; inferences in subjects such as biology, chemistry, or physics would be justified in terms of empirical correlations among variables; and finally, inferences made in a domain of human action might be justified by reference to means-ends relationships.

This mode of analyzing and classifying episodes lends itself to certain logical considerations. For example, those forms of inference which depend upon definitions can be shown to be logically necessary. On the other hand, inferences which are based upon empirical correlations are not necessary but probable. The same claim can be made for inferences in the domain of practice. These are distinctions which are of considerable importance pedagogically and which, if understood by teachers, would by hypothesis obviate many instructional difficulties. For these reasons, the classificatory scheme set forth in the following paragraphs is based primarily upon the kinds of rules and principles used in justification of inferences.

2. Structure of Conditional Inferring Episodes

As we have already indicated, the entry of a conditional inferring episode is made up of two parts. One part consists in a statement of a set of conditions and the other part consists in asking the student to make an inference from the specified conditions. Consider the following entry: 'What happens when you are hypnotized?'. The expression 'when you are hyponotized' gives the conditions and the expression 'what happens' indicates the direction in which the inference is to be made. For correct inferences, if not for incorrect ones, what is inferred can be connected logically with the conditions by some sort of principle. The principle may be explicitly stated, but typically it is only implicitly present. Thus, conditional inferring consists of three elements: a set of given conditions, an inference from these conditions to some further idea or state of affairs, and a principle which can be used to connect logically the conditions and the inferred ideas, states of affairs, and so on. We shall refer to the set of conditions specified in the entry as the antecedent and to that which is inferred from the conditions as the consequent. We shall refer to the principle that is involved either explicitly or implicitly as the connecting principle. As already stated, the connecting principle may be of various kinds. It may be non-empirical -- definitions, rules, or criteria. Or it may be empirical -- correlations among variables or means-ends relations. The relations among these three elements constitute the logical structure of the episode as illustrated by the following model:

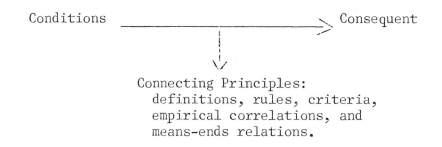

Conditions ————————————> Consequent

Connecting Principles:
   definitions, rules, criteria,
   empirical correlations, and
   means-ends relations.

The following episode illustrates this model. An English class is discussing modifiers.

                  *

Episode 1   T: If you need a modifier to modify a verb, which one is he going to take?

               S: An adverb.

               T: That's how your adverbs run, then?

               S: Yes.

               T: Certainly. Yes. We need this adverb 'badly' to modify this verb 'behave'.

                  *

This episode may be schematized according to the model as follows:

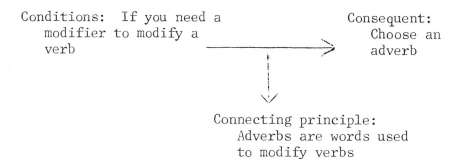

Conditions: If you need a   Consequent:
    modifier to modify a   Choose an
    verb ————————————>   adverb

Connecting principle:
   Adverbs are words used
   to modify verbs

The connecting principle is a definition. This definition tells what adverbs are used for, and it is the basis of the inference that you will choose an adverb if you need a word to modify a verb.

To make an inference from the conditions given in the entry the student need not call up the connecting principle and use it as an element in a deductive argument to derive the consequent. As a matter of fact, he may not be aware of the principle at all. In the so-called discovery method of teaching it is presumed that the student will play his hunches; he will go from the given conditions to some probable consequent without taking account at all of the connecting principle.

In fact, it is believed that should the student take the connecting principle into account, his creativity would be reduced. There is good reason to suppose that in many circumstances this claim is correct. But when a student is asked to give justification for the consequent, he must come back to some sort of principle which enables him to give reasons for his claim that the consequent given by him follows from the given conditions. It can therefore be said that in many cases the connecting principle is of no value in making the inference, but that it may and can always be called for when the inferred consequent itself is to be justified. And the inability of a student to give the relevant principle or to show how it logically connects the conditions and the consequent when called upon to do so reveals a lack of understanding.

While all conditional inferring episodes conform to the foregoing model, there are wide variations in these episodes depending upon the sort of connecting principle involved. We have identified and analyzed the following kinds of inference episodes: systemic, analytic, material, executive, attributive and ascriptive.

3. Systemic Inference Episodes

Episodes of this type are found in content fields such as mathematics and grammar which are based upon either axiomatic principles or rules or both. Such fields are systemic in the sense that their elements constitute a logically interdependent network of definitions and propositions. Because of the logical nature of the system, it is possible to move by inference from one part of the system to another and to carry on an extended discourse without going beyond the system's boundaries.

In conformity with the general model of conditional inferring episodes, the systemic inference episode is composed of three elements: the "systemic idea" supplied in the antecedent, the inferred ideas stated in the consequent, and the relevant rules or definitions of the system by which the consequent may be related to the antecedent. The last element may be explicitly stated in the episode, but this is typically not the case. In episodes of this type, the inferred ideas follow necessarily from the ideas stated in the conditions plus the relevant rules or definitions.

The excerpts given below represent systemic inferences from two different subject matter areas. The first example is taken from a class in geometry.

*

Episode 2 T: And, therefore, since it's a rectangle divided into congruent triangles with the same base and altitude, one triangle will be?

      S: It would be a right triangle.

*

The information given in the antecedent is a rectangle divided into congruent triangles having a common base. What is inferred from this information is that one triangle would be a right triangle. The connecting ideas include the definition of a rectangle as a plain four-sided figure with four right angles. Ordinarily the connecting principle is taken for granted, as in the episode above, but when the student is called upon to offer evidence in support of his inference, he must then appeal to the connecting ideas which were disregarded as the inference was made. To complete the justification of his inference, the student must also show that the consequent follows logically from the antecedent and the connecting ideas.

In the following episode, from a biology class, the eye of the fish is being discussed.

*

Episode 3 T: What do you mean by -- what kind of an eye is it if it is not compound? If it's not compound, what kind is it?

      S: Simple.

      T: Simple.

*

The information given in the antecedent is that the eye is not a compound eye. The student then infers that the eye is a simple one. The justification of the inference involves simple indirect proof where the alternatives are known and all have been eliminated save one. It follows then that the remaining one must be correct. In other words, there are only two kinds of eyes -- simple and compound. If the fish's eye is not compound, then, of course, it must be simple. Were the student asked to give evidence in support of the inference, he would be required to give the foregoing facts and rules.

Inferences made in episodes of this type are appraised by certain epistemic rules as follows: (1) The inference must follow from the antecedent conditions plus the rules and definitions of the system. (2) The systemic rules followed, or definitions employed, must be official, i.e., laid down by authorities in the field. It is characteristic of these episodes that in the context there can be only one correct inference.

4. Analytic Inference Episodes

Episodes of this type are closely related to the systemic form. The use of language is governed by a body of definitions and conventions. Words and statements are related within a language system. An analytic inference is one which takes place within such a language system and follows by definition from information given in the antecedent. That is to say, an examination of the meanings of the terms involved would show that the meaning of the consequent is part of the meaning of the antecedent. Suppose a teacher asks: 'If a person is against free elections, what can we say about his attitude toward democracy?'. Suppose that the student responds by saying 'He would be against democracy, because free elections are part of democracy, and everyone who is against free elections is against democracy.'. It is easy to see that the student's answer follows necessarily from the given information; namely, that the individual in question was against free elections. It follows necessarily because in the student's way of thinking free elections are a part of the definition of the word 'democracy'. So, when one says that he is against free elections he is saying at the same time that he is against democracy. The whole discussion is about the use of words. And whether or not one who is against free elections is also against democracy depends in the final analysis upon how the word 'democracy' is defined. The student's inference does not rest upon fact but rather upon definition. The connecting principle in an analytic episode is always definitional.

The following episode illustrates an analytic inference as found in the classroom. The class is discussing juvenile delinquency and probation.

*

Episode 4   S: Well, I was going to say, <u>doesn't</u> <u>it</u> <u>give</u> <u>you</u> <u>more</u> <u>than</u> <u>a</u> <u>second</u> <u>chance</u>, <u>really</u>, <u>because</u> <u>a</u> <u>lot</u> <u>of</u> <u>those</u> <u>kids</u> <u>get</u> <u>on</u> <u>pro</u><u>bation</u> <u>two,</u> <u>three,</u> <u>four</u> <u>times</u>?

T: Oh yes. I didn't use the term 'second chance' in a very strict meaning that it can have.

S: Oh.

T: It might have had a third, fourth. Maybe we should have said it gives a person another chance.

S: (Speaking simultaneously with teacher) Another chance.

*

It can be seen by analysis that the idea of being on probation more than two times -- three or four times -- includes the idea of the delinquent individual having more than a second chance. This follows from the meanings of the terms 'two' and 'second'. These meanings make it possible to infer that to be given more than a second chance is to be put on probation more than twice.

The epistemic rules governing analytic inference are as follows: (1) The consequent must follow necessarily as the conclusion of a deductive argument, the premises of which are the antecedent statements and the relevant definitions. (2) The meanings of the key words in the inferred consequent and in the antecedent must be clear.

5. Material Inference Episodes

In an episode of this kind the inference is related to the antecedent conditions empirically. The consequent can be logically related to the given conditions by virtue of the fact that there is an empirically established correlation between the two. In the case of material inference, the truth of the consequent does not follow necessarily from the given conditions. For example, consider the statement, 'If it rains, the gridiron will be wet.'. It does not follow necessarily that if it does in fact rain, the gridiron will be wet. It may be that some intervening condition such as a canvas stretched over the football field would prevent the field from being wet even though it rained.

A consideration of some examples of material inference episodes should further clarify the nature of this kind of inference as well as illustrate the diversity of these episodes. In a biology class certain aspects of physiology are being considered.

*

Episode 5 T: Just like you separate your air from your food. When you swallow -- do you ever notice when you swallow, what do you do? You start to swallow -- what stops? Swallow! See what stops?

     S: Breathing does. So it is sort of like that of the fish -- separate by means of muscles.

     T: All right.

*

In this episode, the teacher is trying to establish the fact that if you swallow, you cannot at the same time breathe. He does this by asking the students to try to swallow and to see whether or not they can also breathe while swallowing. A student concludes that breathing stops as one swallows. Given a negative correlation between swallowing and breathing, it is then possible to infer with a high degree of probability in other cases that one has stopped breathing from the fact that he is swallowing. Obviously the connecting principle here is the negative correlation between breathing, on the one hand, and swallowing, on the other. It should be pointed out, however, that even though the negative correlation between swallowing and breathing may be perfect for all known cases, it does not follow necessarily that swallowing will always be attended by not breathing. It is still theoretically possible that some individual may be found who can both swallow and breathe at one and the same time. In other words, there is no logically necessary relationship between swallowing and not breathing. This illustrates one of the characteristics of material inference that distinguishes it from analytic inference, where the relationship is logically necessary.

The next example illustrates a case where the given antecedent condition is of a very general nature and the inference moves to consequents which are described more specifically.

*

Episode 6   S: <u>What</u> <u>happens</u> <u>when</u> <u>you</u> <u>get</u> <u>real</u> <u>nervous</u>?   <u>Do</u> <u>the</u> <u>nerves</u> <u>work</u> <u>harder</u>?   <u>And</u> <u>do</u> <u>they</u> <u>cause</u> <u>more</u> <u>motion</u>?

                 T: Yes. They not only work harder, but they are less controlled. That is, the impulses and responses are more uncontrolled. That is they are carried in and sent out, and through training or education or culture, we try to control them. But if it's a nervous condition, it's the impulses out of control, which means they're affected more rapidly and not as well controlled.

*

The antecedent consists in a condition of nervousness. And the student wishes to know what happens. He then goes on to make inferences from the conditions which he gives and asks the teacher whether he concurs in these inferences or not. The teacher does concur when he says 'Yes'. Then he goes ahead to elaborate. He infers that through education and cultural induction, impulses and responses to them are controlled; but in a nervous condition, the impulses are out of control and the responses of the individual are likewise less controlled. The teacher makes this inference on the basis of an unstated correlation between the general behavior symptoms of nervousness and certain specific physiological occurrences. Had he been challenged by the student to justify the consequent, the teacher would be required to state explicitly the connecting principles which in the episode are present only by implication.

The epistemic rules governing this sort of inference are as follows: (1) There must be significant evidence supporting a correlation between the antecedent and the consequent. (2) There must be no significant evidence disconfirming the correlation. (3) The consequent must follow logically from the conjunction of the antecedent and the connecting principle or correlation.

From a pragmatic standpoint, the person who makes the inference should indicate the strength of the grounds supporting the correlation, by such words as 'likely', 'probable', 'highly probable', etc.

6. Executive Inference Episodes

The antecedent of this sort of episode describes the task to be carried out and the consequent specifies the decisions one would make or the actions one would take to perform the task. In some cases the task is described in terms of goals to be achieved, but in other cases it is described in terms of general actions, and the goal of the task is assumed. Implied but seldom stated in these episodes are the reasons for an individual's decisions and actions. These reasons consist primarily of facts and generalizations relating the individual's actions to the goal as means to ends. While the logical structure of executive inference conforms to the general model, the logical relations among the antecedent conditions, the consequent, and the connecting principles are much looser (lower probability of being correct, etc.) than in the preceding types.

The following examples are typical of executive inference episodes found in the classroom.

*

Episode 7   T: If you were to make a code of ethics for atheletes, what would you include in your code of ethics?   One thing you would include in a code of ethics, perhaps, is ---?

S: I would probably say that there should be no prizes awarded for individual players so that it would split the teamwork -- the team.

*

This episode illustrates a case in which the task is described in terms of a very general act--making a code of ethics. Since no goal for the code is stated, the student in his response supplies a goal he assumes to be desirable; namely, the preservation of teamwork. The action the student decides upon is that of specifying in the code that there shall be no prizes awarded for individual players. As is often the case, the connecting principle is absent, that is to say, no reasons for the action are given.

In the following case, the task to be performed is stated in terms of an end to be produced -- writing an equation.

*

Episode 8

T: Now this point, O, is an equilibrium. So what would we do if we want to write down the equation involving all forces here? What do you do? What technique would you use in handling a problem like this?

S: You'd have to get the point of equilibrium.

T: Okay. We've done that -- point O. What's the next thing you'd do?

S: You'd draw the forces that are acting --

T: All right. We've done that. We've drawn the forces. Now, what's the next thing we'd do?

S: And then we'd have to chart our actions.

T: Okay. You want to draw some actions through here. Now, what would be the logical direction in which to draw the actions?

S: At the parallel to the plane and perpendicular to the point O.

T: All right, right there.

*

The antecedent here is the need to write an equation involving all the forces in equilibrium at a point. The execution of the task consists in a series of actions, each action constituting a step in the development of the equation.

The epistemic rules for appraising executive inferences are as follows: (1) There must be evidence that the proposed action will attain the desired end. This evidence may consist of (a) established generalizations linking the action to the goal as means to ends, or (b) instances in which similar goals were obtained under similar circumstances by similar actions. (2) There must be no substantial evidence indicating that the action will not have the desired result.

If the rules just listed are not observed, there is a good chance that the task will not be successfully completed. Thus, there is a sense in which one can say that an executive inference can be either correct or incorrect. However, an executive inference, even though correct, may be a poor inference. The chosen action may, for example, have undesirable side effects, or there may be alternative actions which are less time consuming, less costly, or less dangerous. For these reasons, rules such as those given above should be supplemented by other rules for determining which action to choose from a number of alternatives, all of which are known to be capable of attaining the desired goal. The factors impinging upon a decision of this type vary greatly from one context to another. Consequently, the following rules are general rather than detailed. (1) The consequences of the action taken as a whole are more desirable or less undesirable than those of any of the alternatives. (2) The action attains the goal more efficiently in terms of time, money, or effort expended than any of the alternatives.

7. Attributive Inference Episodes

Episodes of this type require that an individual infer the properties of an object from its class. To infer the properties of an object from knowledge of its class requires that there be a definitional relation or an established correlation between an object's being in a given class and having a given attribute. Thus, there are three elements in an attributive inference: the object named or classified, the property attributed to the object, and a relation such that the object's belonging to a certain class implies its having a certain property. This sort of episode, therefore, conforms to the general model; the first of the foregoing elements -- the object named or classified -- being the antecedent, the second element -- the property attributed -- being the consequent, and the third element being the connecting principle.

The following examples are typical attributive episodes. The first is from a chemistry class.

*

Episode 9   T: If it's an electrovalent compound, then it would?

S: Dissociate.

T: All right.

*

The student infers that the object having the class name 'electrovalent compound' has the attribute that it dissociates. As is often the case, the definition or correlation by which class membership is related to the attribute is not given. In order to justify the inference that the electrovalent compound would dissociate, the student would have to point out that electrovalent compounds usually exist as crystals composed not of molecules but rather of ions which are held together by affinity for one another. When the crystals are placed in water, the bonds by which the ions are held together in crystalline form are weakened so that the crystal dissociates, or as we say, dissolves in the water. The connecting link between the antecedent condition and the consequent is a series of logically related statements about ions and their behavior.

Consider a further case from a social studies class discussing colonialism and its effects.

*

Episode 10   T: All right. Anything else, here? (Any further effects of colonialism detrimental to the colony)

S: They had to sell their raw materials to the mother country, and they had to buy there also.

T: All right, -- substandard economy -- so that they had to buy what they needed from the mother country.

*

The antecedent conditions are the policy or institution of colonialism and the consequent is that the colony is forced to sell its raw materials to the mother country and to buy there at the same time. In this episode, a limitation is placed on the sorts of inferences which are to be made. The attributes to be inferred from the given conditions are those which are detrimental to the colony. The connecting principles are, first, by definition one of the attributes of colonialism is that a colony must buy and sell from its mother country, and second, such practice results in a substandard economy. From these principles it can be inferred that if an inhabited territory is a colony, it must buy from and sell to the mother country and that it will have a substandard material existence.

Attributive inferences are evaluated by the following epistemic rules: (1) There must be reliable evidence supporting the correlation between class membership and the property attributed to the object. (2) There must be no substantial evidence disconfirming the correlation. (3) If the object's class membership and the attributive property are related by definition, the definition must be accepted by experts in the field to which it belongs.

8. Ascriptive Inference Episodes

In an episode of this type the antecedent conditions contain a description of an event, action, or situation. The consequent indicates the person, thing, or action to which a certain role, status, etc., is to be ascribed. The role, status, etc., that is to be ascribed is specified in the entry of the episode. Determining which person, thing, or action fills the specified role is the task of the person making the inference. To make an ascriptive inference is to employ criteria, at least implicitly. These criteria vary according to the sort of role to be ascribed.

Consideration of two examples will help to clarify the nature of ascriptive inference. In an English class the question of what constitutes murder and how murder differs from homicide and manslaughter is the topic of discussion. The episode is as follows.

*

Episode 11   T: Well, now, if an insane person kills somebody else, who is to blame for the death of the person who was killed?

S: Well, I should think he is.

S_1: Well, you can't blame the person because he has no -- it's not that he didn't have the intention to kill, but because he had no control over what he was doing.

T: Well, you still have to fix the blame somewhere, don't you?

S₂: But that person who did it...

T: Well, yes that's perfectly true. But instead of being sentenced to execution, he might be admitted to a mental institution for the rest of his life, but he still is to blame for the death of the person whose murder he committed even though he was not responsible for what he was doing. He did do it, didn't he?

S₃: Yes, but he wasn't there--all there when he was doing it--I mean, physically, but not mentally.

T: Well, we have to think in terms of cause and effect. The fact that he didn't know what he was doing does not remove the fact that the effect of something that he did was murder. Right?

*

In this example 'an insane person kills somebody' is the action and 'blame for the death' is the role or status which is to be ascribed to some one. The student first ascribes the blame to the insane person. This ascription is challenged by another student. The objection is based upon the fact that the insane person does not meet an important criterion for determining blame, i.e., he had no control over what he was doing. However, the first student's ascription is upheld by the teacher apparently on the basis of the criterion that whoever in fact does the killing is to blame for it, insanity notwithstanding.

The following is the same type of episode, from a class in geometry.

*

Episode 12   T: What is the important idea when you are given three sides of a figure, and the figure is a right triangle? What is the first thing that comes to you when you draw your figure? All right, what?

S: That you have a long one (leg) opposite your right angle.

T: The long side must be your hypotenuse. That's right.

*

Here 'important' is the role being ascribed to the idea that the side opposite the right angle is the hypotenuse. This idea is important in the context in that it is a step in the consideration of the problem.

Chapter XI

EXPLAINING EPISODES

An explanation is sometimes defined as a statement or set of
statements answering a 'why' question. This definition is narrow
because it excludes answers to questions which are normally regarded
as requests for explanations. The answers to such questions as 'What
causes X?', 'How did it happen that X....?', 'How does one do X?',
and 'What made X happen?' are ordinarily taken to be explanations.
Each of these questions could be prefaced by the word 'explain' without
altering the sense of the question. In ordinary usage, one does ask
other persons to 'explain how' and 'explain what' as well as 'why'.
By way of contrast, note that one is more likely to <u>tell</u> when, where,
which, or who than he is to <u>explain</u> when, where, which, or who.

1. Alternative Modes of Analysis

Explaining is frequently conceived to be an activity
intended to fill the gaps in someone's understanding. On this conception, the need for an explanation arises when a person encounters
something which according to his experience was not to be expected,
or which he cannot relate to his experience. It is the function of
explanation to fill the gap between the person's experience and this
new phenomenon. When this gap is filled in, i.e., when the new
phenomenon is associated with the person's experience, he is said to
understand the new phenomenon.

This way of looking at explanation emphasizes an aspect which
is very important from the pedagogical standpoint. It is that
explanations generally are formulated for the purpose of getting some
one to understand something; and to bring about understanding,
explanations must be adapted to the individual's background.

The new phenomenon may be related to various things in the
person's experience, and as the types of things to which the

phenomenon is related differ, so do the types of relationships. Explanations may be classified into several different kinds according to the type of thing the new phenomenon is related to and the type of relationship involved. This approach to the classification of explaining episodes, however, emphasizes the psychological aspects of the process of explaining and overlooks the logical character of explaining. For this reason, this approach to the classification of explaining episodes has not been followed.

Another approach was considered. In every explanation the object, action, event, or state of affairs which is the subject of explanation is somehow related to other actions, objects, events or states of affairs. It is possible to classify explaining episodes according to whether this relation is warranted by empirical generalizations or conventional rules. The nature of the warrant is one of two bases used to determine the subcategories of explanation. However, to classify explanation solely on this basis would obscure many of the distinctions which are pedagogically important. For this reason, we also used the structure of the explanatory operation as the other basis of classification. Thus, the classification of explaining episodes is in part based on the sort of structure which the entries of the episodes require. In some cases the structure is simply that of deduction, in other cases the structure is one of temporal or spatial sequence, and in other cases the structure is that of a loose judgment in which the validity of the explanation might be open to wide objections.

Based on the above considerations the general Explaining category has been broken down into the following subtypes: normative explanation, empirical-subsumptive explanation, judgmental explanation, procedural explanation, sequent explanation, teleological explanation, explanation by consequences, and mechanical explanation.

2. Normative Explanation

Normative explaining consists in giving evidence showing that T_e (subject of explanation -- usually an action or belief) may be subsumed under an established rule or norm. By showing that an action is subsumable under a rule the normative explanation attaches the sanction of that rule to the action.

Some of the rules or norms which are commonly invoked in normative explanations are: laws of political units or of other organizations, rules of manners, games, morality, mathematics, logic, grammar, and rules for correct use of terms, namely definitions. To show that an action is subsumable under a rule, the evidence must identify the action as an instance of the class of things covered by the rule. In sum, the elements of a normative explanation are: (1) T_e, usually an action or belief; (2) a rule or norm under which the action or belief is to be subsumed; and (3) evidence indicating that the action is subsumable by the rule. These elements may be schematized as follows.

Evidence indicating that
the rule applies to the ⟶ T_e (action or belief being
action or belief explained)

Rule or norm

The following episode, from an English class studying grammar, is a paradigm case of normative explaining.

*

Episode 1   T: Why do we use 'shorter'?

S: Because there's only two objects being compared.

T: If there are only two being compared -- if there are just two involved, we use the comparative degree which ends in "er". Many of these adjectives do form their comparison by adding the "er" for the comparative and "est" for the superlative.

*

The action to be explained is expressed by the teacher as using 'shorter'. The rule -- stated loosely by the teacher -- under which this action is to be subsumed is that the comparative degree ending in "er" is used when only two objects are being compared. The evidence -- stated somewhat elliptically by the student -- indicating that the action may be subsumed under this rule is that there are only two objects being compared.

In some normative explanations the rule is cited but the evidence indicating its applicability is omitted. The following episode from a geometry class is such a case.

*

Episode 2

T: How do we know that this angle -- SC -- down here is 120°?

S: Because the opposite angles in a parrallelo -- or a rhombus are equal.

T: The opposites are equal, and of course every two adjacent are -- since it's a parallelogram -- will be supplementary, because this is just another form here. That's right, and since this is a rhombus, it makes them equal, which makes 60 and 60, and therefore an equilateral triangle.

*

The student states the rule under which the belief that angle SC is 120° is to be subsumed, viz., the opposite angles in a parallelogram or a rhombus are equal. He does not cite evidence showing that this rule is applicable in the present case. Some of the relevant evidence, namely, that the figure containing angle SC is a rhombus, is given by the teacher. Still needed to round out the relevant evidence is a statement indicating that the angle opposite angle SC is 120°.

The following episode, from a U. S. history class, is an example of a normative explanation in which students advance conflicting claims and explain them by citing different evidence and involving different definitions.

*

Episode 3

A: What makes this (spoils system) a democratic practice?

S: Well, I don't think it is. But, I mean, it came under the time that all these democratic trends were going on. I don't think it's democratic. I mean it's being kind of -- I don't know what to call it, but I don't think it's being democratic.

S_1: No, I don't think it was democratic either. They thought it was democratic, but maybe we don't have to think it and they just put it in the book because maybe at that time the people thought it was democratic.

S₂: Well, which is the most democratic thing, a person who is forced to choose some group of people that he doesn't necessarily want, or the person who is able to choose anyone he wants?

S: That's not the point! The point is when these people did help, they had to be rewarded with something, and that wasn't a democratic idea. It should have been "Work for the good of the country -- do what's best for the people" instead of "Work for what I can get out of it".

*

In her first utterance, S sets forth the claim that giving government jobs to party followers is not a democratic practice. She explains this claim in the last utterance by indicating that the practice in question is not subsumable under the sort of definition of 'democratic practice' she upholds. According to her definition, a practice involving political action motivated by desire for reward rather than by desire to serve one's country is undemocratic. S₂, on the other hand, does not state a judgment. S₂ explains his opposing judgment (implied not stated) by alluding to a definition to the effect that 'Allowing a person to choose persons he wants is more democratic than forcing him to choose persons he does not necessarily want'. The practice in question is subsumable under this definition.

Another important variation on the normative type of explanation is that in which a rule is cited not to explain a particular belief or action but to serve as a criterion by which to formulate and appraise actions and beliefs in a given domain. The following two examples are representative of this type of explanation. The first is from a biology class studying the classification of animals.

*

Episode 4   T: What's the difference between the scales and the plates as far as the fish is concerned? Why do they call them two different things, or are they the same thing, or is it because of their location that they are different?

S: Well, the plates are on the head instead of on the main part of the body.

T: All right. The main part of the body has the scales and the head, of course, has the plates.

The rule -- essentially a definition -- suggested in this episode is that the term 'plates' refers to things covering the head, and the term 'scales' refers to things covering the body. This rule is not employed here to give sanction to an action or belief, for neither of these is subsumed under the rule. Its function is rather to serve as a guide in future cases where one must determine whether a given portion of the covering of a fish is scales or plates. Since there is no explanation of an action or belief, there might even be some doubt that this is a true case of normative explaining.

The epistemic rules by which normative explanations are appraised are as follows: (1) The rule must be one which is accepted or agreed upon. (2) If empirical, the evidential statements indicating the applicability of the rule must be true; if classificatory, the particular must be an instance of the class covered by the rule according to an accepted definition of the class term. (3) The action or belief being explained must not be a recognized exception to the rule. (4) The action or belief must be logically derivable from the rule in conjunction with the evidence cited.

3. Empirical-Subsumptive Explanation

In explanations of this kind, T_e is shown by evidence to be, or is implied to be, subsumable under an empirical generalization or law. The following diagram indicates the logical structure of this kind of explanation.

Evidence indicating that T_e is an instance of a law or generalization $\longrightarrow$ T_e (event, phenomenon, etc., being explained)

Empirical law or generalization

In some empirical-subsumptive explanations evidence is produced indicating that T_e is an instance covered by an empirical generalization, but the generalization is not explicitly stated. If the student fails to state the generalization, the teacher may supply it, as in the following episode from a biology class.

*

| Episode 5 | T: | Why is that possible? Why can he (insect) do that (see in more than one direction at a time) and you and I can't? |

S: Cause they have more than one lens.

T: They have more than one lens. All right. They have a multitude of lens. A number of lens makes it possible to see in many directions at one time.

*

T_e is the insect's ability to see in more than one direction at a time. The empirical generalization under which T_e is to be subsumed is that animals having eyes with multiple lens are able to see in many directions at one time; it is stated in a loose form by the teacher. The student supplies the evidence -- they have more than one lens -- indicating that T_e may be subsumed under a generalization of the sort given by the teacher.

Not infrequently a generalization serves as evidence and a further generalization, under which T_e is to be subsumed, is implied. Note the following example, again from a biology class.

*

Episode 6   T: What can you tell us about -- we haven't talked about this as yet but we will, I think, in the next chapter -- about cold-blooded and warm-blooded animals. Why is it more cold-blooded animals live in the South than in the North?

S: Because the cold-blooded animals -- don't they have to have the same kind of temperature as their surroundings?

T: They have the same body temperature as their surroundings.

*

T_e is the fact that more cold-blooded animals live in the South than in the North. Offered as evidence by the teacher is the generalization that cold-blooded animals have the same temperature as their surroundings. Implicit in the explanation is a further generalization relating the temperature of a cold-blooded animal to his survival or propagation, under which T_e may be subsumed. A complete statement of the explanation would also include evidence concerning the relative temperatures of the North and South.

Generalizations employed in explanations are not always stated in full, as can be seen from the following example from a physics class.

*

Episode 7   T: What <u>produces</u> <u>all</u> <u>of</u> <u>that</u>? Now, we're not <u>pulling backward on the block</u>. What produces all that?

                S: Friction.

                T: O.K. That's the frictional force.

*

In this example the student says 'friction' as short for a generalization concerning the frictional force acting upon a moving object.

The following are epistemic rules for appraising empirical-subsumptive explanations. (1) The generalization must be capable of yielding predictions which may be confirmed or disconfirmed, and it must not have yielded any significant number of disconfirmed predictions. (2) All empirical evidential statements must be true. (3) That which is being explained must be logically derivable from the generalization in conjunction with the evidential statements.

4. Judgmental Explanation

Closely related to empirical-subsumptive explanation is a kind of explanation which is here called judgmental. In an empirical-subsumptive explanation the relation between the antecedent and consequent, allowing one to explain the consequent by citing the antecedent, is warranted by an extremely probable empirical generalization or law. In judgmental explaining the relation between antecedent and consequent is warranted at most by generalizations of only fairly high probability, for which few of the conditions under which they will hold can be stated. The relation may be warranted only by a somewhat vague and ill-defined body of inductive evidence -- ill-defined in that one does not always know what evidence is relevant.

In judgmental explanation, the antecedent best supported by evidence is selected as being correlated with the consequent, T_e. Judgment must be exercised in deciding what evidence is relevant, in assigning weights to evidence in order to decide among a number of possible antecedents, and in deciding when the evidence is sufficient to warrant the assumption of a relation between a possible antecedent and the consequent. These decisions are not always easy to make, particularly when the consequent is a human action and much of the relevant evidence concerns the character, mood, etc., of the person acting. As is common in most cases of explanation in the classroom, the evidence warranting the explanation is seldom stated unless the explanation is challenged. In schematic form judgmental explanation appears as follows:

Antecedent $\longrightarrow$ T_e (consequent or object of explanation -- action, attitude, state of affairs, etc.)

Evidence

The following example illustrates judgmental explaining.

*

Episode 8   T: The toad is usually characterized by having an ugly, warty skin. <u>Why do you suppose we associate warts with toads</u>?

S: Well, their skin looks like it has a lot of warts on it.

T: All right, their skin looks like it has a lot of warts on it.

*

T_e is our association of warts with toads. Offered to account for it is the antecedent -- "their skin looks like it has a lot of warts on it". In selecting this antecedent the student probably had in mind evidence which might be expressed as follows: Persons ascribe causal efficacy to irrelevant things when they do not know the real cause, particularly when the irrelevant thing has some feature in common with what it supposedly causes. It is reasonable to suppose that a great many people do not know the real cause of warts.

Another example of judgmental explaining is from a history class discussing differences in the U.S. attitudes toward Hawaii, Puerto Rico, and the Philippines.

*

Episode 9   T: Why do you suppose there was that much difference in our attitude toward these three groups -- three island groups?

S_1: Well, in Puerto Rico, in the Philippines the people were pretty illiterate.

T: What about Hawaii -- weren't there a lot of natives in Hawaii?

S_2: Well, not as many as the other two. Well, there were more Americans over there.

T: O.K. The people who had, many of them, been responsible for the revolt against the authorities in Hawaii were American planters. That was a much larger population -- you said if -- there were many illiterates.

*

T_e is the difference among the attitudes of the U.S. government toward the Philippines, Hawaii, and Puerto Rico. Several antecedents are cited as accounting for the difference -- illiteracy of the people in Puerto Rico and the Philippines and the number of Americans in Hawaii. The evidence considered probably included the following: A controlling nation must have a program for illiterate people with a background distinctly different from that of the nation itself which is different from that for literate people with a similar cultural background. Persons responsible for policy in the U.S. government at that time certainly must have realized this principle. Also, it is only natural for a country to treat their own people differently from foreigners.

The foregoing antecedent may have been selected in preference to some alternative antecedent, although this is not likely. For example, the student could have considered as the antecedent the fact that Hawaii was the only island with any significant number of Protestants. Evidence cited in favor of this antecedent could have been an attitude against Catholics and non-Christians holding public office. Weighing this evidence against evidence in support of the other antecedent and finding the other evidence stronger or more convincing, the students could then have judged in favor of the other antecedent.

The student need not always choose between antecedents. If there is more than one antecedent supported by strong evidence, he may give both as accounting for the consequent. This, in fact, is what the student did in the second example. The illiteracy in the Philippines and Puerto Rico together with the large number of Americans in Hawaii was cited as accounting for the consequent.

The following epistemic rules are used to appraise judgment explanations: (1) The statements describing the antecedent which accounts for the consequent, T_e, must at least be plausible. (2) There must be no other antecedent which accounts as well for the consequent. (3) It must be reasonable to suppose that the consequent would not have occurred had the antecedent cited as accounting for the consequent not obtained.

5. Procedural Explanation

To explain procedurally is to state or refer in a general way to a series of actions or operations of which T_e is a result or product. The logical form of such an explanation is exhibited in the following diagram.

Series of operations $\longrightarrow$ T_e (thing
or actions   being explained)

Procedural explanations may be subdivided into two groups: those in which T_e is the result of operations governed by conventional rules, and those in which T_e is a consequence of actions guided by empirical generalizations linking means to ends. Conventional rules are rules whose force derives from the fact that they are implicitly or explicitly agreed upon by a social reference group. Laws, definitions, rules of grammar, rules of a game, rules of mathematics, rules of logic and rules of morality are examples of conventional rules as here defined.

In many explanations of procedures governed by conventional

rules, a single operation is produced to account for T_e. The following example illustrates such a case.

*

Episode 10 T: How do you get it, please? (The answer to a problem)

        S: Well, I took the area -- 28 -- and I multiplied it by 9.

        T: And 9 x 28.

*

The single mathematical operation of multiplying 9 x 28 is presented as accounting for T_e.

Some procedural explanations involve more than one operation, as in the following example.

*

Episode 11 T: How'd you get 5 1/3 please.

        S: Multiplied 2 2/3 x 2 2/3.

        T: How do you multiply? I think you missed a little bit there. You rushed to put it down (and you didn't think too good.) What is 2 2/3?

        S: 8/3.

        T: 8/3, which gives us 8/3 then, times 8/3 times $\sqrt{3}$ and that gives -- cancel if you can John....

        S: It'd be 64 over 9. Oh! It cancels 4 and out...

        T: And it gives you, then, what?

        S: 16 over 9.

        T: 16 over 9 times?

        S: $\sqrt{3}$

        T: $\sqrt{3}$

*

In this example several sub-operations involved in the operation of multiplying 2 2/3 by 2 2/3 are described, e.g., converting 2 2/3 to 8/3 and cancelling. T_e is seen to be the result of these operations.

The procedure by which T_e is produced is not always described. In some explanations of this type the person explaining actually goes through the procedure.

*

Episode 12   T: Sharon, how'd you spell that?

                  S: T-r-a-n-s-l-u-c-e-n-t.

                  T: That's right.

*

Here the student in explaining how to spell 'translucent' actually goes through the procedure of spelling it.

An important variation on procedural explanations of this sort is the case in which going through the procedure has no tangible result. When one explains the procedures for making a cake, refining salt or solving a mathematics problem, he is dealing with procedures having tangible results -- a cake, refined salt, the answer to the problem. When he explains the procedure for displaying sportsmanship, the result -- sportsmanship -- is not tangible. The actions involved in displaying sportsmanship are undertaken for their own value rather than to produce something further such as cake or salt. Performing the actions themselves constitutes sportsmanship, whereas whipping batter does not constitute cake. In the following example the student explains the procedure by which sportsmanship is displayed.

*

Episode 13   T: But let's go back just a little bit. Tell me about how Army and Navy games -- I don't know that this is still true, but how did the Army and Navy teams display sportsmanship at one time?

                S: If the Navy was going to the Army stadium to play, and they didn't have very many rooters, the Army would detail some of their men to go over and root for the Navy.

                T: And they really rooted for the opponents too.

*

The actions involved in the procedure, i.e., sending men to root for the opponent, are carried on for the sake of an intangible result -- sportsmanship.

Epistemic rules for appraising this variety of procedural explanation are: (1) The operation described must be correct as judged by the conventional rules relevant to such operations. (2) Statements reporting particular operations must be true.

Turning now to explanations of procedures governed by empirical rules, we note the following episode from a chemistry class.

*

Episode 14   T: How is it -- boron -- extracted?

S: .... boron dioxide with metallic magnesium?

T: Eleanor?

S_2: It can be extracted by treating calcium borate with sodium carbonate.

T: Richard?

S_3: It is extracted by heating boric oxide and ...

*

The procedures partially described by the students are based on empirical rules relating means to ends. For example, the first student was probably attempting to state the procedure which involves the reduction of boron trioxide with metallic magnesium. This procedure is based on generalizations to the effect that metallic magnesium will displace boron in boron trioxide under certain conditions of temperature and pressure.

In some cases the result for which the procedure is given is the accomplishment of a task not involving the attainment of a product. Consider the following example from a biology class.

*

Episode 15   T: But what about that ancient fish? How did he show those?

S: He showed that they gradually crawled up on land to start the amphibians.

T: Remember the ancient fish? How were they shown? How were the ancient fish shown on that film? How many remember seeing them? What did he show you there in the film?

S: You mean he showed them in pictures, they weren't...

T: In pictures, he had paintings, didn't he, of these ancient fish?

*

Here T_e is the accomplishment of the task of showing the ancient fish. The procedure offered as that which accomplished the task was that of showing pictures (paintings) of the fish. The generalization undergirding the procedure (somewhat trivial in this case) is not stated, but it would probably be a statement to the effect that showing pictures of a thing shows something of what the thing is like.

The epistemic rules for appraising this variety of procedural explanation are: (1) The procedure described must have been used successfully a number of times. (2) None of the circumstances under which the procedure is known to be unsuccessful must be present. (3) If there are steps involved in the procedure, the description must make apparent their proper order.

6. Sequent Explanation

This kind of explanation recounts or refers in general terms to a series of events chronologically ordered. T_e is seen as being the result of these events, or at least as being the next event in the series. Represented in diagrammatic form, the structure of this type of explanation appears as follows:

Series of events _____ then _____→ T_e (event being explained)

The example which follows, from a U.S. history class, is typical of sequent explaining.

*

Episode 16   T: Where Cleveland was unwilling to add territory to the United States, he was almost opposite in his desire to sponsor support for the Monroe Doctrine in Latin America. And what was the situation down in Venezuela which brought that particular thing (invoking the Monroe Doctrine) to a head?

S: Well Britain owned British Guiana and they wanted, I think, 400,000 square miles from Venezuela, and they were disputing about it, and America asked Britain to arbitrate the matter and they wouldn't do it, so Cleveland took it to Congress and they were going to start invoking the Monroe Doctrine.

T: O.K.

*

T_e is Cleveland's invoking the Monroe Doctrine. The student explains this by recounting the events preceding Cleveland's going to the Congress. These events were the British-Venezuelan territory dispute and the British rejection of arbitration.

In this next example, again from a U.S. history class, the events leading up to a given state of affairs are events engineered by a person to bring about the state of affairs.

*

Episode 17 T: Well, how did John Hay, who was Secretary of State, succeed in bringing about the open door policy, Nancy?

       S: Didn't he ask the different countries not to close their ports?

       T: Well, he asked them not to close their ports, or rather to open their ports. Then what else did he -- how did he maneuver it? That's the thing I want. Steve?

      S_2: He sent a duplicate letter to all countries and they all sent back -- said if the other would, why they would. And then he sent letters back saying they all accepted it.

       T: Of course, they didn't know which letter went first, so he got by with that particular maneuver.

*

T_e is the advent of the Open Door Policy. Leading up to this state of affairs was the following sequence of events: Hays sent duplicate letters to the other countries; each of the other countries replied that they would agree if the others would; Hay sent letters saying all had agreed; all did agree; thus the policy was adopted.

Epistemic rules for the appraisal of sequent explanations are as follows: (1) Recognized authorities or competent witnesses must testify that the events did happen in the order mentioned. (2) The events mentioned must be relevant to the event or state of affairs to be explained. (a) The events described in the explanation must involve the same persons or things mentioned in the state of affairs to be explained. (b) It is reasonable to suppose that the event to be explained would not have taken place if the events mentioned in the explanation had not occurred.

7. Teleological Explanation

In a teleological explanation T_e is an action. Explaining
the action involves showing that in performing the action the performer
is acting in a manner consistent with some purpose, intention, or
desire he is pursuing. In its complete form there are four elements in
teleological explanation: T_e, the action; the purpose of the person
acting; evidence indicating that the purpose cited does support the
action being explained, i.e., that persons having the purpose are
likely to perform the action; and evidence indicating that the purpose
is a reasonable one for the person acting to have in light of his
character and the circumstances in which he finds himself. These
elements may be schematized as follows:

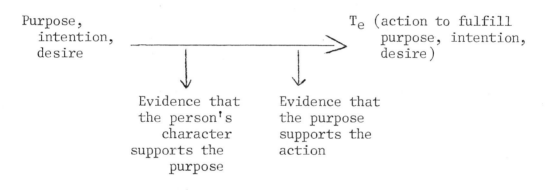

Two distinct kinds of teleological explaining are carried on
in the classroom. In the first, the person explaining supplies the
purpose which he believes accounts for the action. While he may give
evidence concerning the character of the person acting and the circumstances under which the action took place, the explainer does not offer
evidence that the purpose supports the action; he merely assumes that
it does. Consider the following example, from an English class discussing a series of events in a novel.

*

Episode 18   T: Why did he -- Jarvis -- leave it -- room?

               S: To go down and see what was the matter.

               T: All right, he heard the noise, he heard the
                   servant calling and went down there.

*

In this example T_e is the action of leaving the room. The purpose offered in explanation is that Jarvis wanted to go down and see what was the matter. The teacher's final statement concerning Jarvis' hearing the noise and the servant calling constitutes evidence indicating that it is reasonable to suppose that Jarvis had the purpose in question.

In the other sort of teleological explaining, the explainer does not state the purpose for which the action was undertaken. Rather he assumes that the person acting had a given purpose and proceeds to give evidence showing that the action was a likely or reasonable one for the person to take, given his purpose.

The following episode, from a world history class discussing the Boxer's Rebellion in China, illustrates this type of teleological explanation.

*

Episode 19   T: The worst outbreak of the Boxer's Rebellion occurred outside the city, not within the city of Peking. <u>Why would they pick on that particular city</u>?

S: Because it's the main seaport?

T: No, not the main seaport. The main city, but there's another reason. It's not because of the seaport. Anyone else have an idea? Bill?

S_2: Would that be where all these foreign offices were?

T: What's another word for it? It's where the big foreign legations were, that's true. All the leaders of these foreign groups were there. Where would you find them? What city?

S_3: In the capitol.

T: In the capitol. It was the capitol; it's still today the capitol.

*

T_e is the Boxers' "picking on" the city of Peking. The evidence that Peking contained foreign legations relates the action of selecting that city (to pick on) to the purpose of the persons engaged in the rebellion, which was to get the foreigners to change their policies toward China. It is reasonable to demonstrate in the city containing the most foreign officials if one wants to change the policies of foreign nations.

Consider another case from a different subject matter field -- chemistry.

*

Episode 20   T: Why is lead very often used on pipes?

R: It doesn't oxidize or anything.

T: Once it has a coating on why it's the same kind of /material/ outside as .... to protect itself. As long as it is coated, why, then you have no trouble.

*

T_e is the use of lead on pipes, and the evidence that relates T_e to the purpose is information concerning a characteristic of the material used in the action, i.e., that lead does not oxidize.

Epistemic rules for appraising teleological explanations are: (1) The supplied or assumed purpose must be one which it is reasonable to attribute to the person acting on the basis of the person's character and the circumstances under which he is acting. (2) The sentences stating evidence must be true. (3) The evidence must be relevant to the operation of connecting the action and the purpose. Relevant evidence (a) indicates that the probable consequences of the action constitute achieving the purpose, (b) calls attention to some characteristic of the action, the materials employed in the action, or the circumstances in which the action takes place which indicates that the probable consequences will constitute achieving the purpose, or (c) shows that under similar circumstances persons having the purpose usually performed the action.

8. Explanation by Consequences

In this type of explanation one accounts for a phenomenon by relating it to the consequences its presence helps produce. That is to say, one explains the phenomenon by citing its role in a larger pattern of events. An implicit but seldom stated element in such explanations is the evidence showing that the phenomenon does help produce the consequence cited. The following diagram exhibits the logical structure of this type of explanation.

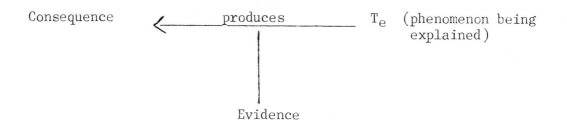

Consequence   ←   produces T_e (phenomenon being explained)

Evidence

        The example cited below illustrates explanation by consequences as found in a discussion in a biology class.

*

Episode 21   T: How do you suppose when the fish opens his mouth -- takes a mouthful of water into it -- closes his mouth and pushes the water out through his gills, doesn't he? Why does it do that? Why does the fish push water out through the opening that's called the 'plate' covering the operculum -- that has openings underneath? Why does he do that?

                  S: To get the air out of the body -- to get the air -- the oxygen out of the water.

                  T: To get the oxygen out of the water. Let's be exact. To get the oxygen out of the...

                  S: Air.

                  T: Air which is dissolved in the water.

*

Here T_e is the fish's pushing water through its gills. The consequence offered to explain this phenomenon is the fish's getting oxygen out of the air present in the water. In the larger pattern of events having to do with the survival of the fish, the role of the fish's pushing water through its gills is that of getting oxygen.

        Not all explanations of this type are found in biology. Note the following example from a U.S. history class discussing the holding of property in the early days of America.

*

Episode 22   S: Why was it important that Americans had...

                  T: That was a question which nobody heard.

                  S: Why was it so important at first that an American had to hold property?

S_1:   Well, he couldn't vote if he didn't.

*

Here T_e is the importance of holding property in early America. The consequence which is given to account for the importance of holding property is that one couldn't vote unless he held property. That is to say, holding property was important because in one's political life it had the role of a requirement for voting.

An epistemic rule for appraising consequence explanations is: the statement relating the phenomenon being explained to a given consequence must have been empirically confirmed in a number of past instances.

9. Mechanical Explanation

A mechanical explanation of T_e -- an ability, pattern of behavior, state of affairs, etc. -- consists in setting forth the steps or phases in the process by which T_e is accomplished. In the few episodes we found, the explanation usually involved showing how certain important elements in a structure work together to accomplish some function. Usually T_e is not some particular which is specifiable as to time and location (as in sequent explaining), but a repeatable pattern of behavior, state of affairs, etc. Mechanical Explanations are most often found in biology classes.

The following episode, from a biology class discussing how fish separate food from water, is a typical example of mechanical explanation.

*

Episode 23   T: How do you suppose the fish can separate the food from the water? They take it into their mouth and they push the water out over their gills in order to get the oxygen. How do you suppose this fish gets anything to eat? Or, do you suppose he just swallows all the water that he takes into his mouth? He'd be pretty full of water if he did that -- and yet he gets his food. How's he do it?

S: Well, when he swallows the water, these gill rakers -- well, most of the water goes back

out the operculum. Well, the gill rakers
filter out all the dirt and the rest of
the matter goes on into his stomach -- and
he doesn't have teeth -- I mean chewing
teeth. He just holds them and he has stomach
acids which dissolve the food material.

*

Here T_e is the fish separating food from water. The student gives the
steps in the process occurring in the fish to accomplish the separation.
The steps given by the student are swallowing the water, most of the
water going back out the operculum, the gill rakers filtering out dirt
and other matter. These steps, in the proper order, are necessary to
the separation of food from water.

In the following episode, from biology, only one structural
element -- a sticky disc -- is given, but this is a necessary element
without which the frog could not climb trees.

*

Episode 24 T: What makes it possible for these frogs to
climb? We call them tree frogs. Why can
they do that climbing -- a problem that we
have?

      S: Well, they have a sticky disc on each toe and
they can climb.

      T: All right. On the film, remember, we saw that
very well.

*

The epistemic rules for appraising mechanical explanations
are: (1) The statements describing the process must be true. (2)
If there are phases or steps involved in the process, the explanation
must make clear the order in which they occur. (3) The relationships
among the phases or steps must be established as accomplishing T_e, with
no significant disconfirmations.

Chapter XII

EVALUATING EPISODES

Evaluation permeates much of our everyday lives. In fact, practically anything can be and is evaluated at some time or another, in some context. This pervasiveness is reflected in the classroom. Although only about five per cent of the episodes we have studied are classified in the Evaluating category, the variety of things evaluated and the terms in which they are evaluated are quite marked, as may be seen in the criteria for classifying entries in Evaluating.

1. The Logical Nature of Evaluating

Because of the contexts, evaluative terms and the variety of things evaluated, it is impossible to give a satisfactory general definition of evaluating which will serve to identify an evaluating episode. But it may be said that such an episode is one in which the student or teacher appraises or rates something, or one in which a value matter is raised in some way, such as to ask whether there is agreement on an issue, answer, etc.

Although many technical distinctions have been made among the various aspects of evaluating, our episodic material justifies distinguishing only four logical elements of evaluating: (1) something such as an object, statement, expression, event, action, or state of affairs -- designated hereafter as T_e for convenience -- to be evaluated; (2) an evaluation of T_e in terms such as good, unjust, false, desirable, etc.; (3) a warrant by which the evaluation is supported, backed, or justified; and (4) facts, called connecting facts, about T_e which show the connection of T_e to the warrant and thereby support its use in evaluating T_e.

These four elements may be represented in diagrammatic form as follows.

Model of Evaluating

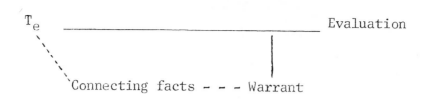

2. Problems of Analysis

The precise character of the logical elements of evaluating and the relations of one element to another depend so greatly on the context in which the evaluation is made that we could not hope to present here an exhaustive or even exclusive classification of the various kinds of evaluating. Rather, we shall present what seem to us to be typical patterns or kinds of evaluation that occur in the classroom, using rather broad and necessarily vague divisions.

Since the analysis is to focus on actual responses in the continuing phase of the episode, our classification must be based on distinctions of some kind in at least one of the four logical elements discussed above.[1] Briefly the rationale for our choice is as follows.

Evaluating episodes vary in the amount of material they contain on each of the four logical elements of evaluating: T_e, the evaluation, the warrant, and the connecting facts. All the episodes contain at least two elements: T_e and the evaluation; many contain only these two elements. In view of this situation, it is tempting to propose these two elements as the basis of classification. Yet it is doubtful that distinctions made in either of these elements could be

---

[1] Not only are many areas and matters of evaluation raised in the classroom, but the ways they are introduced in the entries also vary greatly. Some entries ask directly for evaluations, other entries are less direct: they may ask whether another student agrees, whether something is really or actually the case, etc. Some entries ask for an evaluation, others ask the student merely to affirm or deny a given evaluation. It is possible that this variation in the form of the entry has some logical or pedagogical significance. If so, how much? Does it justify inclusion in the initial efforts toward a classification scheme? Whatever the significance of the variation in entries, we have chosen to ignore these variations in our present analysis.

a sound basis for a logically significant classification scheme. The same is true of connecting facts, since they cannot be stated meaningfully except in the context of a warrant. This leaves distinctions among warrants as the remaining consideration.

Very few episodes contain warrants as such. However, in many episodes facts are stated which are apparently intended to serve as warrants. At first blush the comments in the episode seem more like defending, clarifying, elaborating, or just commenting on the evaluation given. Further analysis, however, discloses that these comments are used as, or function as, warrants. In many contexts, the statement of connecting facts is clearly meant to imply a warrant suitable for the context. In spite of these difficulties, we have chosen the kind of warrant as the most significant basis for our classification scheme. The warrant, as a grounds or backing for the evaluation, is the one logical element most relevant to assessing the correctness of the evaluation, and it is the correctness of responses which has been the main concern in this project.

3. Kinds of Evaluating

The four kinds of evaluating we have analyzed, based on the kinds of warrants, will now be presented, with episodes illustrating each kind.

A. Application of Rules

In this kind of evaluating something is evaluated in terms of whether it conforms to a rule. This rule, then, is the warrant. The rule may be a deductive or mathematical rule, a rule of evidence, a grammatical rule, etc. Evaluating the validity of an argument, the correctness of a mathematical proof, the correctness of sentence structure, and the truth of a statement or set of statements all involve the application of some kind of rule.

There were three sorts of rules involved in these evaluating episodes: formal rules, grammatical rules, and evidential rules (rules of evidence).

1. Formal rules. This kind of evaluating involves both

logical and mathematical rules. Logical rules include the rules of
deduction, the so-called laws of logic (excluded middle, non-contra-
diction, identity), substitution, etc. Mathematical rules include
rules of addition, subtraction, various geometrical theorems, etc.
Application of formal rules is exemplified in evaluating an argument
as valid by applying the well-known rules of deduction, checking each
point of the argument where a deduction is involved.

The few episodes of this kind that involve logical rules are
quite elliptical -- omitting explicit statement of both connecting
facts and warrants -- and even involve erroneous evaluation of arguments
and application of supposedly well-known logical matters. Surprisingly
enough, there were no evaluating episodes which used or referred to
mathematical rules.[2]

The following episode illustrates the use of a logical rule.
The teacher in a sociology class has just reported a statement by
J. Edgar Hoover to the effect that the crime problem is a youth
problem.

*

Episode 1   T: Does that agree with what you think?

S: I read, let's see in the paper, I think it
was a month or two ago where he just con-
tradicted himself because he said that the
teen-agers weren't all at   fault. I mean
that they weren't committing the most crimes,
and that some bad kids were just shoving
around the good kids and that they were all
getting blamed, but the teen-agers weren't
as bad as they thought they were. So, he
wrote that and he wrote this too. He's
just contradicting himself. So he must not
know.

S$_1$:   ....teen-agers, that doesn't mean much.

---

[2] This may be accounted for partly by the kind of entries found in the
mathematics tapes. Typically, the entries do not ask directly for an
evaluation -- e.g., 'What is the correct answer to the third problem?'
-- but rather they ask the student to repeat an operation -- e.g.,
'What is that answer again?' -- so that he sees the mistake himself.

T: In one of the other reports given in 5th period, J. Edgar Hoover was quoted again and he stated that 97% of the teenagers were good law-abiding citizens, which may be on your side, Sue. And I think speaks well for the great majority of teenagers. But it's this other 3% or so that brings the bad name upon the group.

*

In this episode Sue points out a contradiction in two statements apparently made by Hoover, one that teenagers commit the most crimes and the other that they don't. The rule involved here -- not explicitly -- is the so-called "law of noncontradiction."

2. Grammatical rules. This kind of evaluating involves grammatical rules that specify subject-verb agreement, which parts of speech modify others, correct kinds of sentence structure, etc. For example, the adverb 'quickly' is used correctly to modify the verb 'run' in the sentence 'The fox runs quickly'.

These episodes are easy to identify, as seen in the following example from an English class discussing how one part of speech modifies another.

*

Episode 2   T: Anyone want to disagree?
             S: "Good" adds to "employment."
             T: Well, that's true.

*

In this episode the student points out that 'good' modifies 'employment.' The connecting fact, that 'good' is an adjective and 'employment' is a noun, is not brought out explicitly. Also, as with all episodes of this sort the rule -- adjectives modify nouns -- is not stated explicitly, but is fairly clear from the context.

3. Evidential rules. In this kind of evaluating are inductive rules and rules of evidence for establishing the truth of propositions, hypotheses, statements, etc. These evidential rules include Mills' methods, modern statistical methods, and various aspects of scientific methods in general. Evidential rules of course, are not formal in character, as are logical and mathematical rules.

The following episode illustrates this kind of evaluation.

*

Episode 3   T: What's the matter with what he just said?

S: /Mumbles/

T: I can't hear what you're saying.

S: ....really a fallacy.

T: What kind?

S: Hasty generalization.

T: A hasty generalization.

*

Here a student's statement (unfortunately inaudible) prior to this episode is criticized as involving a hasty generalization, i.e., a generalization was made beyond that which would be justified by rules of inductive inference.

B. Comparison with Criteria

      In this kind of evaluation T_e is compared with or is assessed in terms of a criterion or set of criteria.[3] The warrant, then, is the criterion or set of criteria. For example, a good apple has certain criteria such as redness, firmness, a certain range of flavor, etc.; a good automobile has certain criteria such as speed of acceleration, a certain degree of braking power, bright headlights, etc.

      The following episodes illustrate this kind of evaluation.

*

Episode 4   T: Were they able to adequately outfit these men for -- service? Suppose they'd had -- oh let's say 50,000 men that volunteered. Would they have been able to get them ready for service down here in Cuba? Now, the Navy was well-organized and could take care of things. Was the army well-organized?

S: No.

T: No, the quartermaster's -- department was very much behind the ...in their procedures and in their ability to take care of these people. Actually, they didn't have very many summer uniforms, and one of the problems that these men -- these volunteers who went to Florida --

---

[3] For a detailed discussion of this kind of evaluating, considered more broadly, see Urmson, J. O. "On Grading." In Flew, Antony. Logic and Language. 2nd Series. Oxford, England: Basil Blackwell, 1959.

you see, this was coming into spring and into summer, and here they were with winter uniforms and down in semi-tropical territory where it was extremely warm, and the wool uniforms weren't very comfortable. They did not have adequate... much ammunition and while that part of it was more easily remedied than some of the other things, they were certainly not too adequately outfitted in the beginning of the war and could not have stood a tremendous increase of men.

*

Episode 5   S: It doesn't seem to me that the way John Quincy Adams became president wasn't -- sort of what I would feel a fair way.

          T: Well, I was going to ask that of Rick. What is your judgment of ... in '24?

      S_1:   Oh, that the requirement. Well, this country is built so that any man can back anyone he pleases, and it's his privilege to do that, and if he can't do it -- well -- he should be able to even though it doesn't seem right. I mean what're we talking about now?...Adams as president, had power to pick his cabinet, and he should have done it.

*

In episode <u>4</u> the army is evaluated in terms of implied criteria of a well-organized army -- especially the efficiency of the quartermaster's department in supplying uniforms appropriate to the season, in providing adequate ammunition, and provisions for sudden and "tremendous" increase in the size of the army. In episode <u>5</u> the way in which Adams became president is defended as fair by two criteria: our American tradition that any man can back anyone he pleases, and the president can pick his cabinet as he sees fit. However, the student gives no connecting facts showing how the criteria fit this situation.

C.   <u>Appeal to Personal Factors</u>

In this kind of evaluation there is no appeal to objective (suprapersonal) warrants such as rules, norms, standards, criteria, etc. Rather, the evaluation is supported or defended only in terms of a warrant such as personal feelings, likings, desires, preferences, etc. For example, a person considers cauliflower a good food just because he likes it.

Two examples of this kind of evaluation are as follows. In

the first, an English class is discussing a novel about the future of
Africa.

*

Episode 6   T: And this would be desirable? Black supremacy?

S: To him /John Kumal<u>o</u>/ it would. I mean, that's
what he wants--I mean that's what the black
people would want, but...

*

The class in the following example is discussing a mother
encouraging her son to fight back.

*

Episode 7   T: Do you approve of that?

S: Oh, I don't know. I like to fight and wrestle
... and stuff like that. I mean it's all right
if they don't really get hurt--hurt each other
real bad.

*

In episode 6 the warrant for the desirability of black supremacy is
"what the black people would want". In episode 7 a mother encouraging
her son to fight back is approved -- in the first part of the utterance
-- on the basis of the student's own liking of fighting and wrestling.

D. Examination of Consequences

In its simplest form there are two distinct aspects to this
kind of evaluation: the first aspect is the determination of the
consequences or outcome of T_e, where T_e is usually an act, event,
process, practice, custom, etc. The second aspect is evaluating the
consequences or outcome of T_e in terms of one of the other kinds of
evaluation -- application of rules, comparison with criteria, or appeal
to personal factors.[4] This second aspect constitutes the warrant.
For example, spanking may be considered undesirable because the long-
term effects of resentment toward authorities leads to unsocial
behavior.

Although the consequences of T_e may in one sense be considered as connecting facts, thus seemingly reducing this kind of
evaluation to one of the three kinds already presented, we consider

---

[4] For a discussion of this kind of evaluating, see Dewey, John. Theory
of Valuation. Chicago: University of Chicago Press. International
Encyclopedia of Unified Service, Vol. II, No. 4.

the difference important enough to maintain this as a distinct kind of evaluation. Here the characteristics or features of T_e itself are not considered and compared with criteria, as in the case of evaluating by comparison with criteria. Rather, it is the condition or state of affairs brought about by T_e that is considered.

This kind of evaluation is often found in more complex form than that described above. For one thing, the outcome of T_e may have already occurred or it might have been predicted. For another thing, either the intended effect or the actual outcome of T_e may be considered. Finally, T_e itself may be considered only as a means -- and thus not evaluated directly -- or T_e itself might be evaluated directly. In these more complex cases, one must take account of and balance all the factors in the situation to arrive at a sound evaluation of T_e.

The following episodes are concerned with examining consequences.

*

Episode 8 T: <u>Now</u>, <u>do you think that this is effective writing</u>? What does he achieve by doing this?

       S: Well, I think it makes you think when you are just reading through it and not...and this way you have to think whether he is telling the truth or being ironical.

       T: You do respond to this, then? It does provoke something in you?

       S: Yes.

       T: All right.

*

Episode 9 T: Is it fair for an author to use emotional appeal, in which to promote his argument?

       S: I think it definitely is, because if things... appeal, and if you can't get people interested in emotion, then you can't promote a cause. Once you get people interested, then you can appeal to their reason also.

       T: You have to get their attention first by appealing to their emotions?

       S: I think you do.

*

In episode <u>8</u> the writing is called effective because it results in provoking thought, it "makes you think." In episode <u>9</u> the use of emotional appeal in an argument is judged to be fair on the basis of its consequences -- getting people interested in order to appeal to their reason.

4. Deficiencies in Occurrence and Handling
of Evaluating in the Classroom

The following discussion of logical elements not explicitly
expressed in evaluating episodes is to be understood only as logical
criticism, not an evaluation of the teaching from a pedagogical standpoint. Whether or not teaching behavior would have more desirable
effect if it conformed more closely to logical models is an empirical
question beyond the scope of this project. The main concern here is
with a logical analysis of evaluating as it occurs in the classroom.

A. No Warrant Given

In many episodes no warrant at all is given for the
evaluation. In a few cases, however, the warrant is not given in the
evaluating episode itself, but in a later episode, usually in response
to an entry such as 'Well, why do you think that is a just law?',
which would be classified in Explaining.

In each of the following episodes, no warrant is given for
the evaluation. In the first episode the class is discussing the
statistics on crimes by adults and crimes by teenagers.

*

Episode 10   T: You were mentioning that there was nothing
in there to indicate what part was committed
by adults. Were those figures that you give
us, those show the percentages of crimes committed by teenagers? Is that right?

S: Yes.

*

Episode 11   T: If they say that higher wages will cause the
mines to close down, now, what argument could
he use? Higher wages would cause the mines to
close down, therefore, that is why we're not
getting higher wages. Isn't that what the
cause is? Now what argument could he use against
the people who were saying that if they have
to raise the wages, they'll have to close the
mines down? Is it good argument to say "our
poverty is what is keeping the mines going?"
Isn't there a better, more logical argument
against saying the mines will close down if
the wages are higher?

S: You could turn it around, and say that...

T: Well, you're on the right track. Not quite, but keep going.

S: Well, if they don't want a percentage, they want it all. And if they can't get it all, then they -- then they'll close down the mines. Because they don't want just a share of it.

*

In episode 10 the lack of any warrant seems unimportant, since it is fairly obvious. In episode 11, however, no warrant is given for "a better, more logical argument." Since whatever warrant the teacher may have had in mind is not clear from what is said or from the context, the student may be confused, especially since the teacher is using the terms in an unusual sense.

B. Factual Statements with No Warrant

In some episodes, a statement of the connecting facts is given, and no warrant is offered to support the evaluation. In some cases this is fairly satisfactory, since in the particular context the statement of the facts by implication almost provides a warrant. Such was the case with episode 4 -- with the entry, 'Was the army well-organized?' -- given above as an example of 'Comparison with Criteria'.

In other episodes, however, the warrant is omitted, and the facts stated are clearly inadequate to provide or imply a warrant. An example of such an episode is as follows.

*

Episode 12   T: A big jail. This is why the law here is ready, isn't it? And the law is firm and the law is law, so to speak. Is it true?

G: No.

T: No! Things are very lax around here, but the big jail is something that makes the people feel better. All right.

*

C. Inappropriate Warrant

The teacher or student practically never questions or examines critically the warrant given for an evaluation. This may be true even though the criteria are not appropriate. This may be seen clearly in episode 9 -- entry: 'Is it fair for an author to use emotional appeal, in which to promote his argument?'. In this episode the kind of warrant appealed to involves merely the consequences, whereas ordinarily the criteria for 'fair' include much more than this, such as various traditions, taking advantage of weaknesses of people, etc.

Inappropriate criteria, not challenged or in any way questioned by the teacher, may be seen also in the following episode -- from an English class discussing a character in a novel -- which illustrates poor handling of criteria for a moral judgment. Moral judgments are not usually made on the basis of such personal qualities as unlikable, emotional, and being a ham.

*

Episode 13   T: This is a weakness, isn't it?
             B: No.
             T: Would you say he was a bad man?
             B: Yes.
             T: He's not admirable, that's for sure.
             B: He's not completely unlikable.
             T: He's not completely unlikable.
             B: He's pretty emotional.
            B_1: He's a ham.
             T: I think that's fair to say. All right.

*

D. Reliance on Personal Factors

In some episodes evaluative terms are used which require non-personal criteria to support the evaluation. If personal factors are relied on exclusively in such cases, the evaluation clearly is not supported adequately. For example, in episode 6 -- entry: 'And this would be desirable? Black supremacy?' -- the reliance on personal factors seems clearly inadequate, since at least the possible consequences and conflict with strong traditions should be considered. On the other hand, in the following episode from a class discussing statistics on crimes, the use of personal factors seems more suitable.

*

Episode 14   T: Anyone have any question that you'd like to
                  ask Liz about the article she quoted from?
                  <u>Were there any things in there that seemed
                  to you to be rather shocking as far as
                  statistics is concerned that she gave</u>? Were
                  they as you had expected them to be?

              Liz: Well, that 1,000 cars a week, that really
                   shocked me when I discovered that. Can
                   hardly believe that.

*

5. Discussion

We would like to discuss briefly some matters having to do
with the kinds of evaluating we have presented.

A. Moral and Esthetic Evaluation

After examining the foregoing kinds of evaluating, the reader
is likely to wonder what happened to moral and esthetic evaluation.
This requires some comment.

We only have about five episodes which seem to involve moral
evaluation, three of which contain no criteria or facts at all, one
which does but is very unclear, and one which merely states facts which
could be interpreted as reasons or criteria. We have only two episodes
which seem to involve esthetic evaluation, neither of which contained
any criteria. Since we have so little basis for examining the kinds of
evaluation involved in these episodes, we have not considered it sound
or fruitful to analyze them. Furthermore, little seems to be lost if
each of these episodes is placed in one of our present classes. Thus,
in view of these considerations we have not proposed a separate class
for moral or esthetic evaluations. In future work and on the basis of
further evidence, however, we may wish to modify this position
accordingly.

B. Epistemic Rules

The four kinds of evaluating differ significantly with
respect to the epistemic rules for assessing correctness of the
evaluations.

(1) Application of rules. Here the rules which support the

evaluation are the epistemic rules -- e.g., the various deductive rules, mathematical theorems, grammatical rules which form the basis of the category itself.

(2) Comparison with criteria. We have been unable as yet to clarify the epistemic rules in this kind of evaluating. There are, of course, ways of checking or validating these evaluations, such as agreement among experts. Furthermore, if the criteria can be specified in completely non-evaluative terms -- e.g., the criteria for a good apple are specified in terms of size, shape, color, etc. -- then whether T_e satisfies the criteria is essentially decided according to evidential rules.

(3) Appeal to personal factors. There apparently seem to be no epistemic rules for these evaluations, since they are psychological reactions, dispositions, feelings, etc.

(4) Examination of consequences. The first aspect of this kind of evaluating -- determining the consequences of T_e -- is a "factual" or "predictive" matter; here the epistemic rules are evidential rules. The second aspect -- evaluating the consequences of T_e -- reduces to one or more of the other three kinds of evaluating.

It is interesting to note that the first three kinds of evaluating can be arranged on a continuum of the degree of subjectivity or personal factors involved in the kind of warrant. At one end of the continuum, there is little or no subjectivity: the warrant is "completely logical." For example, the validity of an argument depends only upon the logical relations among the premises and the conclusion, and not on the feelings or preferences of any person. At the other end of the continuum, there is a great deal of subjectivity: the warrant consists of personal preferences, likings, cathexes, etc., with no logical rules or objective standards involved. For example, a person thinks boxing is a good sport because he enjoys it.

C. Conflicts among Kinds of Evaluation

Since a thing may be evaluated by any one of the four kinds of evaluating, there are many situations where at least two of the kinds of evaluating are used by different parties, leading to confusion or dispute. For example, in episode 7 two kinds of evaluating appear, with conflicting evaluations as a result.

We know of no general rules or criteria by which it can be decided which is the correct kind of evaluating in any particular situation.

Chapter XIII

OPINING EPISODES

An opining episode is one in which a student is asked for a conclusion concerning what is, was, will be, could be, or would have been the case. It is characteristic of such episodes that the entry gives few, if any, explicit conditions from which the conclusion is to be drawn. The student may have in mind certain facts and beliefs which he does not state and which he would often find difficult to express were he asked to do so. Suppose the entry asks 'Do you think there are living things on Mars?'. The student replies 'Yes, I certainly think there is life there'. The student is taking for granted certain conditions on Mars which he does not state and of which he may not be aware. He presumably holds such conclusions with much less conviction than those he reaches on the basis of evidence of which he is aware and about which he feels certain.

The rendering of an opinion is somewhat similar to conditional inferring. In the latter, the student is asked to supply little if any information beyond that given in the entry. In the case of opining, the student often supplies the evidence upon which he bases an opinion. In many cases the evidence is unavailable. Thus, for example, in the matter of whether there is life on Mars, the evidence upon which one might be willing to assert with a high degree of certainty that life does or does not exist on that planet is actually not accessible. So, one's conviction about the soundness of his opinion may rest also upon certain beliefs about what the evidence is or might conceivably be. These considerations, together with others that will become clear from the discussion which follows, have led us to keep the category of opining separate from the category of conditional inferring.

1. Problems of Analysis

Opining episodes may be analyzed in a number of ways. Several of these were considered and rejected as inadequate for the purpose of making logical distinctions of pedagogical significance.

One method of analysis is to classify episodes according to the sort of thing the opinion is about. Thus one may have classes of opinions about attitudes, intentions, actions, future events, past events, etc. While there are logical differences among some of these opinions, many of them are logically indistinguishable from one another.

A second way of analyzing opining episodes is that of placing them along a continuum varying from judgments based on little or no evidence to judgments based on overwhelming evidence. While such an analysis would no doubt be interesting from a psychological point of view, it gives little insight into the logical differences to be found among opining episodes.

The method of analysis yielding the most useful logical distinctions for our purposes is that of grouping episodes according to the type of relation existing between the evidence and the opinion itself. By classifying episodes according to these relations, it is possible not only to draw useful logical distinctions such as that between empirically and conventionally supported opinions, but also to determine the epistemic rules by which various kinds of opinions may be appraised.

2. The Logical Structure of Opining

Three elements enter into the logical nature of an opining episode: (1) the opinion or conclusion; (2) facts on which the opinion is based; and (3) warrants which determine the relevance of facts and sanction the drawing of a particular conclusion from them. The term 'fact' is used here in a broad sense to refer to any datum selected as relevant to the justification of an opinion. For example, the term may stand for a definition, an unobservable such as a belief, or an observable. Of the three elements only the conclusion is always stated. Facts and warrants, the backing or support for an opinion, are often not given. Thus, the following analysis is more speculative and outlines possibilities more than have previous chapters.

The relations among the three elements above constitute the logical structure of opining. The general form of this structure may be represented as follows:

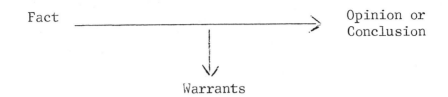

Fact ⟶ Opinion or Conclusion

Warrants

The following episode illustrates the use of this diagram.

*

Episode 1   S: I thought the ability to write with your right or left hand was inherited.

T: No, it can't be inherited. I think it's an acquired trait that we learn.

*

This episode may be diagrammed as follows:

Fact: Every known case of a person writing with his right or left hand has been a case where the person learned to do so. ⟶ Opinion or conclusion: No, it can't be inherited; it's an acquired trait that we learn

Warrant: When every known a is b, conclude that all a's are b.

The various kinds of opining all exhibit this same general structure. They differ widely, however, with regard to the types of warrants relevant to the justification of their conclusions.

3. Analytic Opining

Analytic episodes of this type require that the student determine whether what is correctly described by one term can also be described by a second term. The relevant facts are definitions, and the warrants are logical rules of contradiction and noncontradiction.

The following example, from a social studies class, is a typical example of this kind of opining.

*

Episode 2   T: Well, is democracy necessarily opposed to imperialism?

S: No, they're not opposed to imperialism necessarily, but it's the way that Russia goes about getting her countries that a democracy does not like. Because she takes all...

T: All right. It's all right, then, to have -- it's democratic to have subject peoples, but it's just the way you get them to be subject? Is that what you're saying?

S: No, like the United States has countries under her, but she has them -- she gives them freedoms and things; but Russia -- she doesn't have their -- they don't have any voice in the government or anything, and the United States' colonies do.

T: In other words, it's all right to have people under you if you are kind to them? It's all right to treat people as second class beings if you are kind to them -- just like you are kind to your little dog, or something?

S: No.

T: Feed him regular, pet him a little bit?

S: You're twisting around what I said, though, I said.... You've got me all confused.

*

The student is asked to decide whether any government correctly described as a democracy may also be correctly described as being unopposed to imperialism. The student concludes that a democracy need not be opposed to imperialism. He does not cite definitions of democracy or imperialism to support his opinion. But the teacher attempts to formulate certain aspects of the definition of democracy the student is presupposing, namely, that it is democratic for a nation to have subject peoples if it goes about getting them in the proper way. The student denies holding this view and tries to get across his conception of democracy by contrasting Russia and the United States with respect to their treatment of colonies. Again the teacher attempts to formulate the definition of democracy held by the student, by saying that it is all right for a nation to have subject peoples if it is kind to them. The student protests that he does not subscribe to this view either. It is interesting to note that the student defines neither democracy nor imperialism, although these definitions are to be used in underpinning his judgment. For his part, the teacher disputes the student's implied definition of democracy and ignores the relevance of the student's conception of imperialism to the opinion being given. The warrant linking the facts to the conclusion is not stated. If a warrant were to be supplied, it would be to the effect that two terms are not contradictory if the class of things referred to by one is included in the class of things referred to by the other, and contradictory if one term connotes the presence of an attribute and the other term connotes the absence of it.

In the next episode, a third term, 'scientific thinker', is introduced to support the judgment that the first two terms are not applicable to the same person.

*

Episode 3   T: Could a rationalizing person be a straight thinker?

S: I don't believe...

T: Yes?

S_1: No, in a movie it said it was the opposite of a scientific thinker.

T: Yes.

S_2: I'd say he wouldn't because he should -- the person who had this idea that theirs is the best, they should listen to the other ideas first, before they express their views.

T: Rationalizing is believing just what you want to believe or thinking just what you want to think regardless of what the situation might be. As you said, it's the opposite of scientific thinking.

*

To support his opinion that a person to whom the term rationalizer is applicable cannot be described as a straight thinker S_1 equates the term 'straight thinker' with 'scientific thinker'; he then appeals to the authority of a movie to establish that 'rationalizer' and 'scientific thinker' are opposites. S_2 goes on to point out that the rationalizer

would think his ideas best without listening to others first. The
teacher closes the episode by defining 'rationalizing'. The other
definitions on which the judgment is based -- definitions of 'straight
thinking' and 'scientific thinking' -- are not stated; nor are the
warrants relating the definitional facts to the opinion.

Appraising the adequacy of an analytic opinion involves
appraising the facts and warrants which back the opinion. The
epistemic rules relevant to the appraisal of an analytic opinion are:
(1) The definitions of the terms involved must be official, or, if
they are not official, there must be good reasons for accepting them.
(2) The rule which serves as a warrant must be an accepted convention.

4. Empirical Opining

An opinion of this sort is one whose supporting facts are
observable, and whose warrant relates these facts to other empirical
facts or to an empirical generalization. Two types of empirical opining episodes are distinguishable, correlational and frequency.

Correlational Opining. In this type, two events or states
of affairs are cited and the student must decide whether or not the
second event will occur when the first occurs. An opinion of this
sort is backed by observable facts and by warrants which are correlations among variables. The relevant facts and warrants are seldom
stated in the episode unless the opinion is challenged.

Below is a typical episode of this sort which occurred in a
biology class. The kinds of atmospheres conducive to animal life are
being discussed.

*

Episode 4   T: Nitrogen, could a man or animal live in that?
               Class: Uh-huh.

*

The students conclude that there is a positive correlation between the
two states of affairs -- a man's being in an atmosphere of nitrogen
and a man's being alive. Neither the facts nor the warrants to support
this opinion are stated. It is not possible to decide what facts and

warrants a student would choose to back his opinion if required to do
so, since various facts and warrants may be invoked.

A student may select as facts certain instances of the
correlation about which he is making the judgment and use as a warrant
some inductive policy relating instances to empirical generalizations.
This sort of support may be called direct backing. Consider this
episode as an example.

*

Episode 5   S: You require energy to stay awake, don't you?

                T: Yes.

*

If direct backing were supplied for this opinion, the episode in
schematic form would look like this.

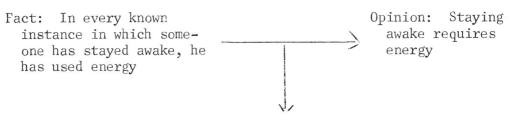

Fact: In every known instance in which someone has stayed awake, he has used energy   ⟶   Opinion: Staying awake requires energy

Warrant: Whenever every known case of _a_ is _b_, all _a_'s are _b_.

Thus, the facts and warrants to be appraised in direct backing are
observables and empirical generalizations, respectively.

In addition, there are various sorts of indirect backing for
an opinion. One in particular is worth mentioning since it illustrates
the use of an empirical generalization of considerably less generality
than that found in direct backing. In this case, the fact used to
support the opinion is that one of the events or states of affairs is
an instance of a larger class of events or states of affairs. The
warrant is a generalization relating this larger class of things to
the particular event or state of affairs. Such backing, if supplied
for the opining episode above, would look like this:

Fact: The state of being awake is a state of physical tension   ⟶   Opinion: Energy is required to stay awake

Warrant: Energy is consumed in any state of physical tension

The list of possible items of backing which may have to be weighed in the course of appraising correlational opinions includes observable data, subsumption of certain events or states of affairs under larger classes, and empirical correlations of varying degrees of generality and abstraction.

Frequency Opining. In an empirical opining episode of this type the student must conclude that a given event does or does not occur with a given frequency. Depending upon the sorts of facts the student may consider, he may employ one or more of several different types of empirical warrants in justifying his opinion. He may employ a policy for drawing statistical inferences. Or he may employ empirical generalizations or probability correlations, such as: every occurrence of a increases the probability that b will occur; or, if a occurs, b is likely to occur.

In the following episode, from a social studies class discussing crime statistics, the given frequency is described only in very vague terms.

*

Episode 6 T: You think that there are just a lot of cases like that (cases in which innocent people are sent to prison)?

     S: I imagine that there's quite a few.

     S_1: I bet there are quite a few innocent people in prison that shouldn't be there.

     S_2: But what should be in there is a lot of good...

*

The student must decide whether the event -- innocent people are sent to prison -- occurs "a lot." The judgment of the frequency is "quite a few." No facts or warrants supporting the judgment are cited.

The student could provide backing for this opinion in two ways. He could let the frequency remain vague and cite equally vague facts and warrants. For example, he might cite as relevant the fact that he knows of several cases in which prisoners have been proved innocent of the charges for which they were in prison. He might then use as a warrant a vague generalization to the effect that when one knows of several cases of innocent people being sent to prison, there are apt to be a lot of such cases about which he does not know. A second way the student could provide backing for this opinion would be to remove its vagueness by stipulating what range of numerically described frequencies correspond to "a lot." Having done this, the student could use numerically quantified data as facts and precise rules of statistical inference as warrants supporting his opinion.

In the next episode the frequency is not explicitly stated.

*

Episode 7   S: Do you think the Russians buy these magazines and take apart these pictures and see what's all in these flash parts and so forth?

T: No. You mean buy things like that?

S: Because in the reflection in that thing it showed the whole laboratory and the rest. Or do you think they are pretty careful about that showing?

T: Probably most of it they already know, but I'm sure that they do buy these and have them on record. It's just that much further evidence or illustration.

*

Here the question implies that one must determine whether the Russians at least sometimes buy these magazines and take apart the pictures. The student states some of the relevant facts, namely that the picture shows the whole laboratory. Other facts and warrants to support the opinion are not given.

The examination of frequency opining has revealed two new items of backing which may have to be appraised in assessing the adequacy of empirical opinions. These are first, policies for drawing statistical inferences, and, second, probability generalizations, that is, generalizations to the effect that the occurrence of a increases the probability that b will occur.

The epistemic rules relevant to the appraisal of empirical opinions are as follows: (1) Statements recording observable data must be true. (2) The subsumption of an event or state of affairs under a class must be a correct classification according to accepted criteria. (3) The generalizations must have yielded a significant number of confirmed predictions and there must have been no

significant number of disconfirming instances. (4) Statistical
inference policies must have supported a number of confirmed predictions.

5. Interpretive Opining

Here the student is asked to form an opinion about an unobservable such as a person's idea, attitude, emotion, or intention.
These opinions are backed by statements of observable facts and by
warrants which are not empirical generalizations, but rules for inter-
preting observable data and determining what unobservable states the
data signify. These warrants state in a very general way the kind of
data relevant to determining whether or not such state exists, and the
person rendering the opinion exercises considerable discretion in
deciding whether or not any particular datum is relevant, or the
available evidence is sufficient to support the conclusion.

In the following example, from a literature class discussing
a novel by Graham Greene, the students are asked to give an opinion
about the attitude of one of the characters.

*

Episode 8   T: Incidentally, what does Father Rank think about
Scobie? Could you say? He just made one comment,
but this is enough.

S: Well, he thought ... (Several students talking
together)

T: Just one person at a time now.

S_1: Well, he thinks that all he does is right,
doesn't he?

T: All right. Regardless of what he knows people
say about Scobie, Father Rank says, I think I'd
have to see it to believe it or something like
that.

S_2: No, he says that "If it's Scobie, don't worry
about it."

T: "If it's Scobie, don't worry about it." That's
it. In other words, Scobie does everything right.
This is what he meant to imply. So Father Rank
has a purpose in the novel. Any further questions
on this?

*

The student concludes that Father Rank's attitude concerning Scobie is that he thinks anything that Scobie does is right. Evidence in support of this opinion may be drawn from all of Father Rank's actions and statements concerning Scobie found in the novel. Cited as relevant to the conclusion are Father Rank's statements to the effect that he would not believe the things said about Scobie until he saw them, and his view that "If it's Scobie, don't worry about it." No warrants linking these facts to the conclusion are given.

If the warrant were stated it would be somewhat as follows: persons who indicate that they will not believe anything bad about person X, and that X's being involved in something is grounds for one's not being concerned about it, have an attitude toward X of thinking that anything X does is right. This is a peculiar warrant, and almost certainly does not do justice to the warrant actually used by the student. Interpretive warrants are extremely complex involving vague sorts of rules combining elements of custom, intuition, and commonsense. It is not surprising it is difficult to make them explicit.

In the second example, from the same discussion as the last example, an opinion concerning the author's intention is given.

*

Episode 9   T: Does he (the author) want you to condone Scobie's crime?

           S: Well, no.

           S_1: He's not interested...

           S_2: I think he wants to say, you'd do the same thing too.

           T: All right.

*

The students are to decide whether or not the author's intention is to lead the reader to condone Scobie's crime. Relevant evidence may include not only passages in the novel, but also information about the author's moral code and literary techniques, as well as statements he may have made concerning his intention in regard to this point. The conclusion in this case is that the author does not want the reader to condone the crime. Neither facts nor warrants are cited in support of the opinion.

In the following episode, from a history class, the student gives an opinion concerning the fears of a historical figure.

*

Episode 10 T: Well, South Carolina didn't get what they expected to get -- the aid they expected to get from any of the southern states. So, <u>what do you suppose that Jackson's followers were afraid of?</u>

        S: That they would be forced to give aid from the government, that the government would force them to...

       S_1: Well, they were afraid of an open split in the Democratic ranks.

*

The opinion is that the followers of Jackson were afraid of an open split in the Democratic party. While some of the evidence relevant to the opinion is stated by the teacher, the student giving the opinion cites none himself.

Because the warrants involved in an interpretive opinion tend to be vague, subject to myriad exceptions, and limited in a way such that small changes in the facts would render them inapplicable, it is not unusual to find conflicting opinions backed by almost identical sets of facts. This is not to deny the possibility of assessing the adequacy of interpretive opinions. However, the epistemic rules appraising such opinions are, understandably, vague. Such rules include the following: (1) All factual statements must be true. (2) A warrant is not to be employed if there is another one which is more generally accepted or which appeals more to commonsense and links a greater number of facts to the conclusion.

6. Counterfactual Opining

To render a counterfactual opinion one decides what point of view, attitude, or action a person would have taken had he faced a given issue which in fact he did not face. Such an opinion consists of two subsidiary opinions: one concerning the interests, ideals, and practices followed by the person, and another concerning what point of view with regard to an issue is consistent with such interests, ideals, and practices. The first subsidiary opinion may be supported by facts concerning the overt behavior and verbal expressions of the person together with the rather vague and limited warrants by which observable behavior is linked to psychological states and practices. In the second subsidiary opinion, the relevant facts consist in the person's interests, etc., and the warrants connecting these with the conclusion concerning the person's point of view or action with regard to the question at issue. The warrants connecting the person's interest, ideals, etc., to the action or point of view he would take may be: (1) statements of means-ends relations between actions and interests, (2) statements of class inclusion -- that the action is a case of engaging in the practice or that holding the point of view on the issue is a case of holding a given ideal, (3) statements of generalizations to the effect that persons with interest, etc., similar to those of the person in question have held similar views.

The logical structure of counterfactual opining may be diagrammed as follows:

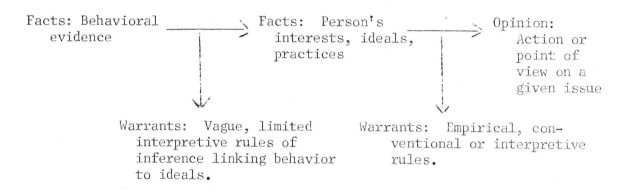

This type of opining is complicated both by the fact that there are no clear criteria for determining what issues are similar, and by the fact that every person follows many ideals, interests, and practices some of which would support his having one viewpoint on a given issue and some of which would support his taking an opposing viewpoint. This being the case, a student's opinion rests in large measure upon his discretion in deciding which ideals were most important to the person and which issues are to be counted as similar.

The following example is typical of counterfactual opining.

*

Episode 11   T: I will just say offhand -- just to see how
well you agree with me -- we know that
Jackson was against giving federal funds for
highways. <u>How would you say Hamilton would
stand on that point?</u>

S: Well, I think he would be in favor of it, because
that would give the federal government more power.

T: That's the way I would look at it.

*

The student must decide what sort of stand Hamilton would take on an
issue he did not face: namely, that of giving federal funds for
highways. The opinion given is that he would have been in favor of it.
A warrant given in support of the opinion is that giving federal funds
for highways would give the federal government more power. The student
is assuming that enhancing federal power was one of Hamilton's chief
interests.

In the next example, the student's realization that
Jefferson's interests and ideals could have led to conflicting view-
points is perhaps the source of her hesitation.

*

Episode 12   T: The Tariff Act. <u>Do you think that Jefferson
would have agreed with South Carolina or not
-- on the issue of nullifying the Tariff Act?</u>

S: Wait.

T: Hard to say, isn't it?

S: No, no I don't think so.

*

After hesitating the student somehow decides which of Jefferson's
interests and ideals were most important to him, then concludes that
Jefferson would not have agreed with South Carolina in its attempt to
nullify the Tariff Act.

A counterfactual judgment is most often a loose sort of judgment which cannot be appraised as correct or incorrect. In general, a
counterfactual judgment can be appraised as more or less adequate according to the breadth of the evidence considered. The first subsidiary
judgment may be appraised by the epistemic rules for interpretive
opining. The second subsidiary judgment, depending upon the type of
warrant employed, may be assessed by the epistemic rules for analytic,
empirical, or interpretive opining.

PART   THREE

Chapter XIV

LOGIC, LANGUAGE, AND PSYCHOLOGY[1]

From the very beginning of our efforts to analyze classroom
discourse into units and to classify them logically, we have been confronted by a pervasive problem -- a problem stemming from the fact that
logical operations are verbally expressed in a number of ways. In this
section, we shall treat this problem briefly and then go on to deal
with a second problem which we have faced from time to time, namely,
the need for a broader conception of both psychology of thinking and
logic in the study of teaching behavior. In the long run the latter
problem may turn out to be the more significant problem of the two,
but it is nevertheless the one which we are less prepared to discuss at
this time.

1. Logic-Language Relations

Language is used for many purposes. Some of these are clearly
logical in character, e.g., to define a term, to carry on a course of
reasoning, and to prove the truth of propositions. Other purposes are
clearly nonlogical in character, e.g., to give orders, to make promises,
and to express admiration. Still other purposes are neither clearly
logical nor clearly nonlogical, e.g., to communicate information.
Because language must be flexible and efficient enough to serve so many
purposes, it does not achieve any one purpose as well as it might were
it designed only to achieve that one purpose. Because of this multi-
purpose nature of language, some features of verbal behavior are puzz-
ling when one is attempting to study logical operations as expressed in
such behavior.

We encountered a number of distinct but related problems
arising from such features of verbal behavior. These problems arose in

---

[1] Adapted from Meux, Milton and Smith, B. Othanel. Logical dimensions
of teaching behavior. To appear as a chapter in a book on teacher
competence, edited by Bruce Biddle and Nicholas Fattu.

our selection and clarification of a unit of classroom discourse, in the construction of logical categories, and in the internal analysis of the logic of episodes. Presumably these problems would have been easier to solve if we had had at our disposal a complete catalog of relations between logic and language in different contexts. Perhaps it is not even possible to develop a complete catalog of these relations. Nevertheless it should prove interesting to note a few examples. The first two examples have to do with logical operations and linguistic forms; the last two with the effect of context on the kind of logical operation called for by a sentence.

(1) Different logical operations can be called for with one kind of linguistic form. For example, entries such as 'What is the horse?', 'What is the reason?', and 'What is the method?' all have the form 'What is the X?'. Yet each calls for a different logical operation. 'What is the horse?' calls for a definition or an identifying description of the animal horse. 'What is the reason?' calls for an explanation or a justification of some act. 'What is the method?' calls for an illustration or description of the method by which something is to be accomplished -- making an object, conducting an experiment, etc. Thus it is clear that in this linguistic form a key word in the entry -- the word designated by X -- determines the kind of logical operation called for.

(2) One kind of logical operation can be called for equally well with entries of varying linguistic forms. For example, the entries 'What does axon mean?', 'How is the term axon defined?', and 'The definition of axon is what?' are all alike in one important respect. Each one calls for a definition of the term 'axon'. This is quite clear, even though the terms and grammatical forms of the entries are not alike.

(3) In some cases, it is possible to determine from the linguistic form alone, i.e., without benefit of the context, the particular logical operation called for by the entry. For example, responses to entries such as 'What is the definition of imperialism?' and 'How does one explain the increased temperature in that flask?' involve logical operations which conform closely to those taught in

works on logic and philosophy of science. It is quite easy to identify the logical operations called for by such entries.

(4) A very different kind of example is to be found in linguistic forms which do not clearly call for one and only one kind of logical operation, but may be interpreted as calling for any one of two or three kinds of logical operations. The kind of logical operation required by such a linguistic form cannot usually be decided uniquely without considering the context, which typically is sufficient to determine the kind of operation. An example of such a linguistic form is the entry 'How would you define cultural lag?'. This entry can be taken either as asking for the definition of 'cultural lag' -- as would be the case in most contexts -- or as asking for the method of defining to be used.

2. Logic-Psychology Relations

Our study has been conducted as a natural history form of inquiry, involving observation, description, and classification of logical behavior in the classroom. The basic criterion of logical behavior may be considered to be that it is governable by logical rules, those we have called epistemic rules. Thus, different kinds of logical rules form the basis for the different categories developed. This approach resulted in the following problems.

In developing our logical categories, we attempted to make the basis of each category the kind of rule a person would follow in forming an ideal response to the entry. Thus, in an ideal response to one kind of Defining entry, the standard rules of definition would govern the response -- rules such as making the definiens and definiendum the same scope, not repeating in the definiens what is in the definiendum (noncircularity), and not defining the term by what it does not denote (nonnegativity).

The responses to some entries, however, did not seem clearly to be of a kind which could be governed by rules. The Opining and Describing categories contain the best examples of this kind of entry.

For example, the response to an Opining entry such as 'What will the next generation say about President Eisenhower's administration?' does not seem to be governable by well-formulated rules. For example, it seems to make more sense to speak of defining well than it does to speak of opining well. A similar point can be made with respect to that part of the Describing category, -- reported only briefly in Chapter V -- concerned with describing or reporting one's feelings. What rules, e.g., does one follow in answering questions such as 'How do you feel about snakes?' and 'Do you have headaches?'?

The question then arises as to whether all our categories are logical ones -- in the sense of the ideal response to an entry in the category being governable by rules. Are some of them more psychological in character? How governable by rules does behavior have to be to be considered logical?

The extent to which a student governs his responses to an entry by following a rule or a set of rules depends on whether rules are formulated that are appropriate to answer the entry, on whether the student knows the rules, and on how well he can apply his knowledge of the rules to respond to the entry.

Even the available rules of definition -- one of the best-studied logical operations -- are not sufficient to govern completely the response to every situation calling for a definition. Since the main purpose of a definition is to make clear to the recipient of the definition what a term means, the teacher must judge the appropriateness of a definition he is about to give to the class. He must consider the age, knowledge, and other characteristics of the students in judging which formulation of the definition is to be the most effective for this particular class. There seem to be no well-formulated rules for every aspect of this procedure.[2]

On the other hand, even in responding to Opining entries the student is guided by some rules, though they are quite general. For example, take the case of the Opining entry cited above -- 'What will the next generation say about President Eisenhower's administration?'.

---

[2] There is some doubt as to whether it is even possible to formulate rules for every situation that could arise.

The rules to be followed in this case are those involved in examining what historians have said about presidents with beliefs and conduct similar to Eisenhower's, about presidents confronted with similar circumstances, etc.

By the same token, responses to some evaluating entries seem less governable by rules than responses to defining entries, yet more governable by rules than responses to some opining entries. A similar point can be made about the other categories.

The foregoing discussion suggests that there might be a rough continuum on which the categories can be arranged, a continuum defined by the extent to which an ideal response to an entry in the category is governable by rules. On this basis, it could be said that some of our categories are more logical than others. They are the categories containing entries whose responses are governable by rules to a greater extent than are responses to entries in other categories.

Finally, we would like to emphasize more directly that we were hindered throughout our investigation by present narrow conceptions of the nature, scope, and method of both the fields of logic and psychology, and within psychology especially the psychology of thinking. The effect of these conceptions has been to preclude the availability of solutions to some of our most general and pervasive problems, solutions which might have been available under broader conceptions of these fields. We shall indicate briefly how the present conceptions could be broadened, some examples of recent trends toward such broadened conceptions, and then how such conceptions could have helped us in our work.

Logic could be broadened in two ways: one would be the investigation of logical operations as they appear in ordinary language, operations such as defining, describing, and explaining; the other would be the comparative investigation of patterns of reasoning and argument used in various fields such as mathematics, physics, biology, law, ethics, and esthetics. A trend toward such a broadened conception of logic is illustrated in the works of Toulmin,[3] Jensen,[4] and

[3] Toulmin, Stephan E. The Uses of Argument. Cambridge, England: Cambridge University Press, 1958.

[4] Jensen, O. C. The Nature of Legal Argument. Oxford: Basil Blackwell, 1957.

Hart and Honore.[5]

Such a conception of logic would be helpful in identifying more accurately the kinds of logical operations that occur in the classroom. It would also help us by providing a greater variety of logical forms -- e.g., kinds of argument used in everyday life -- that we could use as standards to assess classroom discourse. In fact, Toulmin's work[6] on the structure of practical arguments was quite helpful in the logical analysis of episodes, especially in the Explaining and Evaluating categories.

The psychology of thinking could be broadened by (1) distinguishing and investigating different kinds of logical vs. non-logical behavior; (2) determining the extent to which rule-following is an accurate description of logical behavior, and if so, the various kinds of rules that are followed; (3) determining the relative roles of rule-following and imagination in various kinds of thinking, especially logical behavior; and (4) identifying the various processes and abilities associated with performance and learning of various kinds of logical behavior (defining, describing, explaining, etc.).

Guilford's recent work[7,8] illustrates a trend toward a broadened conception of the psychology of thinking, although not incorporating all the elements outlined above. For example, he has proposed psychological interpretations of logical behavior such as deduction and induction. He has also included evaluating as one of his

---

[5] Hart, H. L. A., and Honore, A. M. Causation in the Law. Oxford: Clarendon Press, 1959.

[6] ibid.

[7] Guilford, J. P. "Three faces of intellect." The American Psychologist, XIV, pp. 469-479.

[8] Guilford, J. P., and Merrifield, P. R. "The structure of intellect model: its uses and implications." Reports from the Psychological Laboratory, No. 24, Los Angeles: University of Southern California, 1960.

operations, which is similar in some ways to our concept of logical behavior, especially our Evaluating category. And his products -- especially classes and relations -- are essentially descriptive concepts of logic. Unfortunately, however, we were unable to use Guilford's system because it does not include sufficient detail in the description and classification of the kinds of logical behavior we have found in the classroom.

A broadened conception of the psychology of thinking along the lines indicated -- e.g., the description of kinds of logical behavior in terms of kinds of rules followed, if that should turn out to be appropriate -- could have helped our work in especially three ways: (1) the developing of logical categories for the episodes along the lines of the kinds of rules actually followed; (2) analyzing ways in which the teacher monitors his own behavior and that of the students; and (3) providing the basis for techniques of improving the teacher's monitoring of himself and of the students.

SUGGESTED READINGS

General

Flanders, Ned A. "Analyzing teacher behavior." Educational
        Leadership, December 1961, 19, 173, ff.

Henle, Mary. "On the relation between logic and thinking."
        Psychological Review, July 1962, 69, 366-378.

Toulmin, Stephan E. The Uses of Argument. Cambridge: Cambridge
        University Press, 1958.

Wilson, John. Language and the Pursuit of Truth. Cambridge:
        Cambridge University Press, 1958.

Unpublished Dissertations

Aschner, Mary Jane. The Analysis of Classroom Discourse: A Method
        and its Uses. University of Illinois, 1959. (Ph.D.)

Ennis, Robert H. The Development of a Critical Thinking Test.
        University of Illinois, 1958. (Ph.D.)

Nuthall, Graham A. Analysis of Teaching and Pupil Thinking in the
        Classroom. University of New Zealand, 1962. (M.A.)

Definition and Classification

Black, Max. Critical Thinking. 2nd edition. New York: Prentice-
        Hall, Inc., 1952. (Chapter 11)

Bruner, Jerome S., Goodnow, Jaqueline J., and Austin, George A.
        A Study of Thinking. New York: John Wiley & Sons, Inc.,
        1956.

Cohen, Morris R., and Ernest Nagel. An Introduction to Logic and
        Scientific Method. New York: Harcourt, Brace, & Co., 1934.
        Chapter 12: Classification and Definition, pp. 223-244.

Hospers, John. An Introduction to Philosophical Analysis. New York:
        Prentice-Hall, Inc., 1953.

Scriven, Michael. "Definitions, explanations and theories."
        Minnesota Studies, Vol. 2 (1958) pp. 99-195.

Simpson, George Gaylord. "The Principles of classification and a
        classification of mammals." Bulletin of the American Museum
        of Natural History, 1945, 85, 1-350. Especially Part 1:
        Principles of Taxonomy, pp. 1-33.

Designating

Austin, J. L. "How to talk -- some simple ways." In Philosophical Papers. London: Oxford University Press, 1961, pp. 181-200.

Quine, Willard Van Orman. Word and Object. New York: The Technology Press and John Wiley and Sons, Inc., 1960.

Russell, Bertrand. "Descriptions." In his Introduction to Mathematical Philosophy. London: George Allen and Unwin, Ltd., 1919. Pp. 167-180. Reprinted in Leonard Linsky (ed.). Semantics and the Philosophy of Language. Urbana: University of Illinois Press, 1952. Pp. 95-108.

Conditional Inferring

Copi, Irving M. Introduction to Logic. New York: The Macmillan Company, 1953. Pp. 229-236, pp. 333-349. 2nd edition, 1961, pp. 245-52.

Little, Winston W., Wilson, Harold, and Moore, Edgar W. Applied Logic. Boston: Houghton Mifflin, 1955.

Explaining

Hempel, Carl G. and Oppenheim, Paul. "The logic of explanation." In Feigl, Herbert and Brodbeck, May (eds.). Readings in the Philosophy of Science. New York: Appleton-Century-Crofts, Inc., 1953. Pp. 319-352.

Peters, R. S. The Concept of Motivation. London: Routledge and Kegan Paul, 1960. Chapter 1.

Scriven, Michael. "Truisms as the grounds for historical explanations." In Gardiner, Patrick (ed.). Theories of History. Glencoe, Illinois: The Free Press, 1959. Pp. 443-475.

Swift, Leonard F. "Explanation." In Smith, B. Othanel and Ennis, Robert H. (eds.) Language and Concepts in Education. Chicago: Rand McNally & Company, 1961. Pp. 179-194.

Evaluating

Dewey, John. Theory of Valuation. Chicago: University of Chicago Press, 1939.

Stevenson, Charles L. Ethics and Language. New Haven: Yale University Press, 1944.

Evaluating
(Continued)

Urmson, John D. "On grading." In Flew, Antony G. N. Logic and
Language (2nd series). Oxford, England: Basil Blackwell,
1953, pp. 159-186.

Opining

Austin, J. L. "Other minds." In Flew, Antony G. N. Logic and
Language (2nd series). Oxford: Basil Blackwell, 1953,
pp. 123-158. Also in Austin's Philosophical Papers, 1961,
pp. 44-84.

Black, Max. Critical Thinking. 2nd edition. New York: Prentice-
Hall, Inc., 1952. Chapter 13: The Grounds of Belief.

Diesing, Paul. Reason in Society. Urbana: University of Illinois
Press, 1962.

Appendix 1

SCHOOLS, SUBJECT AREAS, AND TEACHERS

A. Selection of Schools. Because of the time and cost
entailed in making and transcribing tape recordings, we were able to
record the discourse of only seventeen classrooms, representing five
schools in different communities. These schools were selected in two
ways. Two of the schools had recently participated in a project on
the improvement of critical thinking conducted under the auspices of
the Illinois Curriculum Program. We were able to enlist their assist-
ance in this project. The cooperation of the remaining three schools
was secured, in accordance with University policy, through the Office
of the Coordinator of Public School and University Articulation. This
Office made contact with certain schools by letter and telephone. The
letter described the project's purpose and then went on to give
specific details as follows:

1. Each teacher should be selected from one of the four subject fields
    of English, mathematics, science, and social studies.

2. Select the teachers on the basis of our own judgment of their
    competence as teachers. Teacher participation in this project
    would be voluntary, of course. Three out of the four teachers
    you select should be, in your judgment, teachers of high ability
    -- in other words, from among the best teachers on your staff.
    The fourth teacher selected should be one of average competence
    in your judgment. If you object to selecting an average teacher,
    the fourth teacher also may be one of high ability.

3. Teachers whose classes are to be taped will be given the following
    facts about the recordings:

    (a) The teacher's work is merely to be observed and described.
         No evaluation whatsoever is to be made of any teacher's teach-
         ing or of the conduct of his or her classroom activities.
         This is a fact to be stressed, since some of the teachers
         might work under taping conditions with self-consciousness
         and tensions which knowledge of this fact would dispel.

    (b) Teachers, classes, and schools will remain anonymous on the

tapes and on the verbatim transcriptions of these tapes,
being identified thereon only by code letters and numbers.
Only project staff members may listen to these tapes.

(c) Individual teachers, schools, and cooperating officials will
be officially and gratefully credited for their part in this
research on the final report of this project when it is
published.

(d) To record a class session requires two individuals to handle
equipment and to record the non-verbal context of the proceedings. The project staff has found that the presence of these
individuals (graduate students on the project staff) has
created no discernible disturbance or disruption of classroom activity. After the first day, their presence was
generally taken for granted and the normal atmosphere of
the class reasserted itself.

The letter then asks each superintendent for a different com-
bination of good and average teachers of the various subject areas and
grade levels.

We sought schools located in different sorts of communities,
though we did not include communities in which the average expenditure
per pupil was in the lower third of the schools of Illinois. The five
public high schools finally selected differed significantly in a
number of ways.

School A is located in a suburb which until recent years was
composed almost exclusively of business and professional interests.
However, the last few years have seen an increasing number of working
class people moving into the larger and older houses which are being
converted into multi-family dwellings. The school district includes a
few light industries. The town has about 85,000 inhabitants. Table 1
shows that this school expends more per pupil than 97 per cent of the
public high schools of Illinois.

School B is located in a suburban, residential, rapidly
expanding community with a middle-class population in 1957 of about
60,000. It has a few light industries and is the national head-
quarters of a large insurance company. As shown in Table 1 below,

this community spent an above-average amount of money per pupil: four hundred sixty-six dollars per child in average daily attendance. This is higher than 83 per cent of the public high schools of Illinois.

The district of school C includes a large Air Force Base which has several training courses for maintenance and plane crews. The town's population is estimated at about 25,000. Armed Forces families account for about half of the school population. There are no industries in the town. The school district includes some farm area. Its high school expenditure per pupil was about average for the State of Illinois.

School D is located in a rural town of 7,000. There are only one or two very small manufacturing plants in town. The school district covers a considerable rural area and the pupils are about equally divided between town and country. Its school expenditure per pupil was a little less than average for the State of Illinois.

School E is in industrial and coal mining city which has about 40,000 people. The school is, as in the other four cases, the only public high school in the school district. Its expenditure per child was slightly less than average for the State of Illinois.

Table 1. Average daily attendance and expenditure per pupil, 1953-1954.*

School	Average Daily Attendance	Expenditure per pupil in average daily attendance	Percentile Rank (Expenditure per pupil in average daily attendance
A	2812	$ 636.00	97
B	2804	466.00	83
C	453	354.00	50**
D	550	307.00	48**
E	1737	302.00	48

* The latest figures available at the time the schools were selected.

** These figures are estimates and are within 5 per cent of the correct ranking.

To sum up, these schools have a wide range of community backgrounds. One school is in a middle-class suburb; another school is attended largely by professional-class children. A third is located in an industrial town. Of the two schools which are in rural communities one has a large transient population. Two schools were significantly better supported financially than the other three: 97 and 83 percentiles against 50, 48 and 48 percentiles. In fact, the annual cost per pupil in School A was over twice as much as that of either School D or E.

B. Selection of Subject Areas. The question of the subjects in which to record class discussion, and at what grade levels, was answered in part by the purpose of our study and in part by what was available to us in the schools assisting us. Since we were studying the logic of teaching, it was to be expected that those subjects which emphasize didactic discourse and concept achievement would be most appropriate. This criterion ruled out subjects placing primary emphasis upon the development of skills such as those found in typing, physical education, and the like. In addition, we were interested in comparing the logic of teaching among the conventional content subjects such as history and science. This led us to eliminate those subjects sometimes referred to as vocational such as agriculture and home economics. The availability of subjects and teachers also restricted our choices. For example, it was necessary in one school to tape a physiology instead of a biology class. We had to omit the taping of tenth grade English altogether because the scheduled teacher wished to drop out when the procedures of recording were described. The subject fields finally chosen for recordings were English, mathematics, science, and social studies including history.

Since the logical operations involved in teaching may vary, either in form or detail, from one grade to another, it seemed desirable to distribute the recordings by grades as well as by subjects. We therefore decided to record the subjects for each of the four high school grades. The only exceptions were eleventh and twelfth grade mathematics. These were excluded because of the difficulty of recording the type of symbolic operations usually found in these courses. Our subsequent experience with the interpretation of recording in ninth grade algebra justified this decision. As shown in Table 2, seventeen different teachers were recorded. All together we taped five consecutive class periods per teacher or a total of 85 class sessions.

Table 2.   Summary of Subjects and
Grade Levels Recorded.

	9th grade	10th grade	11th grade	12th grade	Totals
English	1		1	1	3
Mathematics	2*	1			3
Science	1**	1	2	1	5
History-Social Studies***	1	1	2	2	6
Totals	5	3	5	4	17

* The tapes for these classes could not be used because the amount of seat work rendered them unintelligible.
** The tapes for this class were inaudible.
*** Including a class in sociology and one in a Core Program.

The question of how much of a teacher's classroom discourse to record, and whether to concentrate the recording in a brief period of time or to distribute it over a month, semester, or year, is one which we considered at some length. It could be argued that spot recordings over a semester or year would be more representative of a teacher's work than an equal number of recordings taken consecutively. It would appear that spot recordings would tend to cancel out the effects of variations of content within a course and of changes in style of teaching from one topic to another. These are very cogent reasons. Nevertheless, we decided to make five consecutive recordings per teacher. For one thing, such recordings would provide continuity in the teaching of a topic over a period of days. In this way, we would obtain the sort of context useful in a logical analysis. For another thing, consecutive recording is easier to schedule and less disruptive of school routine. These are major considerations when the cooperation of a public school is being sought. Moreover, consecutive recording is less costly in time and money, especially when the schools -- as in the case of two with which we worked -- are a considerable distance away.

C. Establishing Rapport with Teachers. The teachers whose classes were to be recorded were selected, as we have already indicated, by the superintendent or principal or both. Of course, this was not the case for the two schools which had been connected with the previous study of instruction in critical thinking. In these schools, the teachers were selected by the curriculum coordinator in consultation with a project staff member.

The validity of a recording depends upon the confidence of the teacher in those who make the recording and upon his understanding of the purposes and procedures of the taping. For this reason a meeting was arranged with the teachers selected in each school. The purposes and procedures of the project were thoroughly explained. We assured the teachers that the project was for scientific purposes only, that all tapes were to be treated anonymously, and that in no event would the classroom work of a teacher be evaluated. Furthermore, we stressed the importance of each teacher following his normal way of doing things during the recordings. We also endeavored to make clear to the teachers, as well as to the superintendent and principal, that no one should volunteer if being recorded would engender anxiety or otherwise bring about personal discomfort while teaching. Three teachers in two different schools decided not to proceed with the taping, although they had been selected by their administrators.

To further increase the chances of having classroom teaching as near normal as possible, we told the interested teachers that we wanted no more class preparation than they would ordinarily make, that they should teach the normal content in their accustomed manner, and in general to do whatever they normally do in the classroom.

As a further step to prevent modification of regular class-room procedures, we chose weeks which were unbroken by holidays or major school events. That pupils are usually ill-prepared for serious classroom work when a major athletic event is imminent is universally recognized. Also, we chose weeks which were not too near either end of the marking period. We did this to avoid class sessions which were merely introductory or which contained reviewing for major tests.

Another precaution was to have the teachers inform their classes during the week preceding the recordings that the class was to be recorded, explaining why the recordings were to be made. To further insure minimum disturbance we requested that the classrooms remain unaltered physically in any way.

Finally, when we arrived to take the recordings, we set up our equipment as quickly and as unobtrusively as possible. Our tapes did not have to be changed or stopped during class time. In most classes we were seated before the pupils got there.

Appendix 2

TAPING AND TRANSCRIBING PROCEDURES

An important problem was to secure a record of as much as possible of what occurs in the classroom. Tape recordings can reproduce only the sounds of the classroom. But often a facial expression, a gesture, pointing or nodding is essential to understanding the speaker exactly. We had no facilities for making a record of facial expressions and nods. However, we were able to make a record of gestures and points in some cases. In addition, a record was made of the physical contents and arrangement of the classroom, the size of the class, the materials used, etc. Finally, we found it advisable to note the causes of extra-verbal sounds such as footsteps and machines. All of these things were noted so that we might refer to these sources while making subsequent analyses of the classroom discourse.

To record these non-aural aspects a member of the project staff was seated in the back of the room with the machine operator. This observer secured the bibliographic data on all books used in class, the assignments given, and all materials used by students in preparing their reports as well as all dittoed material used in classroom discussion. The observer also made a record of bibliographic information on pictures used in class and on all audio-visual materials. Drawings were made of laboratory equipment used in experiments or demonstrations, and calculations and drawings made on the blackboard were also reproduced. Whenever possible, the observer noted the referent when anyone pointed to something in class discussion and did not name it, using instead the expressions "this", "that", "these", "those", "they", "it", etc. The seating arrangement and the position of other items in the classroom were noted, and insofar as possible the first names of the students and their positions in the room were listed in case future analyses were to find such factors to be important.

The recording equipment consisted of a tape recorder running at 3-3/4 feet per second with a 7-inch reel of tape. We had a volume unit (VU") meter installed in place of the "recording level eye" in

order to better control the lower volumes. A pair of headphones was
also used for a direct aural check of the recording while it was being
made. Three semidirectional microphones were used, each with its own
adjustable stand. A felt pad to lessen the pickup of jarring noises
was placed under each microphone stand. The three microphones fed into
a microphone mixer which had individual volume controls and two amplification stages. This device enabled the person recording to turn on
only the microphone closest to the person speaking. This did much to
increase the intelligibility of the voice by decreasing background
noise.

It was thought before the recordings were made that it would
be sufficient for the purposes of analysis merely to listen to the
recordings as they were played back. But it immediately became obvious
that an adequate comprehension of the logical structure of the
discussion could not be secured this way. Further, it was found that
discussion of the details of the taped discourse was nearly impossible
when only the tape itself and the observer's records were available
for reference. And, in addition, it was found that comprehending the
voices and what they were saying through a rather steady veil of noise
caused by such things as chalk hitting the blackboard, persons walking,
and the normal movement and whisperings of students was not achieved except
through a great deal of concentration. This made it very difficult to
think constructively about what was being said.

It thus was necessary to transcribe the tapes onto paper.
Our technique was to listen and listen again, and to copy down accurately
what we heard. Some words and phrases would be unintelligible to the
transcriber. In such cases, he or she would try to make a guess at
what was being said and would put the guess in brackets.

The transcriber's rough draft was gone over by a staff
member who was actually present in the classroom at the time the recording was made. This individual audited the tape recordings, checking
for accuracy and omissions, and trying to improve on or confirm the
transcriber's guess in cases of borderline intelligibility. He also
supplied the referents, whenever possible, for expressions referring
to the blackboard, to demonstration materials, and the like, and

referred the reader to the appropriate place in the observer's records where diagrams, charts, etc., were reproduced. In cases where the student or teacher quoted anything, the auditor would check the source and get the exact page number for the benefit of the analyst who might later need these things.

The completed transcriptions were put on ditto stencils. Anonymity was maintained with a coding system.

A number of conventions had to be devised for writing down the voices and sounds on the tapes. Dashes were used instead of commas wherever the speaker's pause or hesitation or voice tone did not conform to the punctuated form. The length of longer pauses was indicated in brackets. Voice stress was indicated by underlining. If there was doubt about what the word or words were, they would be put in brackets and prefaced with a question mark, e.g., " ?cerebellum ".

The flow of discussion was divided on the page into utterances which were typed as paragraphs and numbered for convenient reference. (By an utterance we mean the record of the verbal behavior of one individual, at one point or another, in a verbal exchange with one or more individuals.) By breaking up the pages of transcripts in this way we facilitate our later analyses. The teachers' utterances were labeled with "T". Wherever possible the pupils' utterances were identified by first names; otherwise the symbols B (boy) and G (girl) were used.

Appendix 3

CRITERIA FOR CLASSIFYING ENTRIES

1. Defining

   1.1 Criteria and Examples

      1.11 A term is given and the definition, meaning, use, or what we understand by the term is explicitly asked for.

         1.111 What does the word "pons" mean?

         1.112 What's the definition of felony?

         1.113 Couldn't "well" be used as a judgment, exclamation?

         1.114 How would you define that (crime)?

      1.12 A term is given, and the entry asks (implicitly) what the referent of the term is.

         1.121 What is the midbrain?

         1.122 What is a cablegram?

         1.123 What is nationalism?

      1.13 The name of a person or any object, place, or event having a grammatically proper name is given, and the entry asks who he (she) is (was) or what it is.

         1.131 Who was John Hay?

         1.132 Who is John Adams?

         1.133 What is the Monroe Doctrine?

      1.14 A term or expression is given, and the entry asks for a symbol or other expression that takes the place of it. This type of definition involves a shorthand expression. The shorthand expression is given, and the longer expression is asked for, or vice versa.

         1.141 What is the symbol for time?

         1.142 $\underline{S}$ means what?

         1.143 Is $\underline{h}$ the height?

         1.144 $\underline{p}$ means what in the formula?

2. Describing

   2.1 Criteria and Examples

      2.11 The entry asks what is (was) happening, what happened, has been happening, had happened, etc.

         2.111 What's happening in South Africa now?

         2.112 What happened with the Independence?

2.12 The entry asks for an indefinite description -- can you tell us about so and so, what can you tell us about so and so, what about so and so, how about so and so.

  2.121 Can you tell us anything about the schools of New Zealand?
  2.122 What can you tell us about the amoeba?
  2.123 What else can you tell us about the nematode?
  2.124 What about the skin of the frog?
  2.125 How about the surface of the moon?
  2.126 Anyone add anything to that (discussion of boron)?

2.13 The entry asks about the purposes, aim, or function of something.

  2.131 What else does the pupil of the eye regulate?
  2.132 What are some of the functions of the liver?
  2.133 What is the aim of the triple A?
  2.134 What are nouns supposed to do?
  2.135 What does the governor on a motor do?
  2.136 What are we supposed to find out?

2.14 The entry asks explicitly what the relationship is between two or more things. The word "relationship", "related", or "relations" appears in the question.

  2.141 What is the relationship between the big dipper and the north star?
  2.142 How is spelling ability related to reading ability?

2.15 The entry asks what something (object, word, institution, etc.) is used for, or the uses of it, etc.

  2.151 What is another use for hydrogen?
  2.152 What is police power used for?
  2.153 What are some of the uses of marble?

2.16 The entry asks what something (individual, object, institution, etc.) did, was doing, what was done with something, what they did, etc. (If the question asks the person addressed what he does, did, has done, etc., it should be placed in 2.27 rather than here.)

  2.161 What had Wilson succeeded in doing before the war broke out?

  2.162 Did the U. S. go in and take the territory?

  2.163 What did they do with it (treaty agreement)?

2.17 The entry asks about the form, appearance, composition, etc., of something.

  2.171 What does a landau look like?

  2.172 How about the form of a lamella?

2.173 What is lampas made of?

2.174 What was that scene like?

2.18 The entry asks what was found <u>out</u> by someone who is not a member of the class. (If the question asks the person addressed what he found out, e.g., 'What did <u>you</u> find out,' etc., it belongs in 2.29.)

    2.181 What did Darwin find out about the emotions of man?

    2.182 What did the main character discover about himself?

2.19 The entry asks what the properties or characteristics of something are; whether something ever had or now has a particular property.

    2.191 Anyone have any other properties of chlorine?

    2.192 What are some of the physical and chemical properties of iron?

    2.193 What are some of the characteristics of John Marin's paintings?

    2.194 Did man ever have scales?

    2.195 What else is characteristic of the reptile?

    2.196 What do the whales have?

2.20 The entry asks what is the problem of something (animal, person, nation, etc.)

    2.201 What was one of the first problems faced by the Constitutional Convention?

    2.202 What are the problems of the polar bear?

    2.203 Can you name one of the problems Washington faced as a general?

2.21 The entry asks where - where something comes from, where it is located, where it gets its name, etc., where something was done, where it is found, and the like. (Questions which ask where something was discussed or talked about in the course belong in 2.28)

    2.211 Where are the kidneys located?

    2.212 Where did Booker T. Washington get his first name?

    2.213 He wasn't born in Salem, Illinois, was he?

    2.214 Where is Singapore?

2.22 The entry asks when - when something happened, what time it occurred, etc.

    2.221 Do you know what time it was (that Cleveland

served as President)?

2.222 When was the Spanish Armada destroyed?

2.23 The entry asks explicitly for a description. The word "describe" is used in the entry.

2.231 Will you describe the way the main character looked?

2.232 How would you describe the landing of a plane?

2.24 The entry asks how many there is of something, or how long (in a temporal sense or otherwise) something is, and for a numerical value of the area, volume, valence, etc., of a particular something. All questions asking for numerical value of variables or constants go here.

2.241 How many bones are there in the human skeleton?

2.242 How long did the Civil War last?

2.243 The area of the triangle is?

2.244 The sum of the squares equals what amount?

2.245 What is the valence of the (SO_4) radical?

2.246 What is the altitude in this triangle?

2.247 What is the size of that angle?

2.25 The entry asks how the person addressed or the class at large feels (felt), whether or what he (it) understands, what he (it) thinks of, etc.

2.251 Did you like that piece of music?

2.252 Do you ever feel moody?

2.253 Understand (an explanation in a physics problem)?

2.26 The entry asks either the person addressed or the entire class what he (it) notices, has seen or heard, or whether he (it) has read about something, what he (it) learned, etc.

2.261 What do you notice about the fish in the aquarium?

2.262 Have you ever heard of the snowbird?

2.27 The entry asks the person addressed what he does, has done, what he has or has had.

2.271 Do you have headaches?

2.272 Did you ever handle snakes?

2.28 The entry asks what the source of information is, (not what's contained in the source), where (but not what) something was talked about, where one found out about something, etc.

2.281 Where did you learn about the principle of flotation?

2.282 Were you there when the speaker told about the origin of coal?

2.283 What page is that on?

2.29 The entry asks the person addressed what he found out about something. (If the entry asks what was found out by someone who is not a member of the class, it belongs in 2.18.)

2.291 What did you find out about race horses?

2.292 What have you discovered about the way to extract potassium?

2.30 The entry asks what to do, or what the means are, to reach or attain certain ends.

2.301 What does one do to grow unblemished peaches?

2.302 What must we do to find the volume of a cylinder?

2.31 The entry asks whether something exists.

2.311 Does Japan have a king?

2.312 Are there vestigial structures in the human body?

2.32 The entry asks whether (but not by what means) something is changing, has changed, etc.

2.321 Is the earth's surface becoming smaller?

3. Designating

3.1 Criteria and Examples

3.11 The entry may ask for any one of the following: for an example or instance, for either one or some members of a set of things, for something else about an object (abstract or concrete) already introduced, for other groups or types of things than those already mentioned. Entries of this type usually contain such words as "example", "one", "some", "a" or "an", "another", "other", "what else". They never ask, explicitly or implicitly, for all members or for a particular member of a set of things. (Entries which ask for examples or instances of reasons, beliefs, agreements, and the like are to be placed in 4 rather than here.)

3.111 Give me another type of highway accident.

3.112 What is an example of words spelled alike but pronounced differently?

3.113 Can you think of any other types of government?

3.114 Give me a substance that dissolves in water.

3.115 Name some words which have the same form for both plural and singular.

3.116 What else is heavily restricted by tariff?

3.12   The entry gives a set or class of things, and asks that all members of it be named, listed, or enumerated. This type of question differs from those in 3.11 in that it requires implicitly or explicitly, that <u>all</u> rather than some members of the class be named. (Questions which ask for the mere listing of reasons, beliefs, etc., should be placed in 4 rather than here.)

    3.121 What are the parts of speech?

    3.122 Which states did Wilson speak in during his first campaign?

    3.123 What are the different parts of the heart?

    3.124 Name the components in that diagram.

    3.125 What are the races of man?

3.13   The entry gives a particular class or group of things, or else a particular object. (concrete or abstract), such as a word, a line (in a geometrical figure), a biological entity, and it requires that these be specified by name.

    3.131 What would you find next to the nucleus of the cell?

    3.132 What is the longest bone in the human body?

    3.133 Which part of the brain is the lowest?

    3.134 Which word is to be modified?

3.14   The entry describes or suggests a particular person, a character, social group, institution, and it requires that these be identified by name. (Same as in 3.13 except that persons, social groups, and institutions are involved.)

    3.141 Who made the "Cross of Gold" speech?

    3.142 What is the lower house in New Zealand?

    3.143 Whom did they select for the campaign manager?

    3.144 Which group of people supported the revolution?

3.15   The entry asks <u>explicitly</u> for the name of something or for what it is <u>called</u>.

    3.151 Do you know what "strike breakers" are called?

    3.152 What was the name of the man who nominated Harding?

    3.153 What do we call animals which suckle their young?

    3.154 Can you recall the name of the hero (in the play)?

    3.155 What is the technical name for the junco?

4. Stating

4.1 Criteria and Examples

4.11 The entry asks any one of the following: What is (was) deduced, inferred, concluded, decided, recommended, believed, or what are the issues, criticisms, obligations, etc.

    4.111 What criticism did they make of Harding's administration?

    4.112 Does anyone recall the decision reached at the conference?

    4.113 Our conclusion is what?

    4.114 What were Cleveland's obligations on assuming office the second time?

4.12 The entry asks implicitly or explicitly for a formula, equation, rules, (theorems, principles, etc.) when not used to explain.

    4.121 Do figures have to be the same size to be congruent?

    4.122 What is the formula for the area of a square?

    4.123 Newton's law of gravity -- what is it?

    4.124 The area of a triangle must always be what?

4.13 The entry asks for one or more steps or phases in the solving of a problem.

    4.131 What is the first step in the proof?

    4.132 What is the next thing that comes to your mind (in solving a problem)?

4.14 The entry asks the person addressed what answer (solution) he got, whether he has the answer or not, etc.

    4.141 What (solution) have you got?

    4.142 Did you get the answer?

    4.143 Which answer did you get?

4.15 The entry asks or directs the students to practice a given exercise (either repetitive or involving the use of principles to make choices among alternatives) or to give corrections of errors made by fellow students. (Invitations or commands to do or to carry on discussions or to work on problems belong in 13.13 rather than here.)

    4.151 Give us a correction on that.

    4.152 Read these sentences and use the correct verb form in the blanks.

    4.153 Use this word (swiftly) in a sentence.

    4.154 Give me a comparison of these two colors.

5. Reporting

  5.1 Criteria and Examples

5.11 The entry asks for account of what is said about something in a document, book, text, etc., or what is shown on TV, etc.

    5.111 Did the text say anything about Hamilton's economic plan?

    5.112 What did the treaty say about the rights of the Indians?

5.12 The entry asks that the information given in the text, etc., about a problem be stated.

    5.121 Tell us what is given.

    5.122 What do we have given?

5.13 The entry asks for a summary or a review, for what an individual recalls about the class work, and the like.

    5.131 Sum up what we have been doing.

    5.132 What did we say about the public control of business?

    5.133 What do you remember about Jackson's attitude toward the bank?

6. Substituting

  6.1 Criteria and Examples

    6.11 The entry asks or directs the student to multiply, substitute, etc.

      6.111 Multiply it for him.

      6.112 Substitute for us in this equation.

    6.12 The entry asks or directs the students to simplify an expression, etc.

      6.121 Simplify it for us.

7. Evaluating

Perhaps the most reliable (but not completely dependable) verbal cue to these entries is the occurrence of such words as "bad", "good", "mistake", "right", "safe", "true", "freedom", "strong", "new".

  7.1 Criteria and Examples

    7.11 The entry asks whether the action (decision, feeling, etc.) of an individual or group is right, just, democratic, strong, etc.

      7.111 Do you think President Truman did right when he removed General MacArthur?

      7.112 Was the sit-down strike a sensible thing?

    7.12 The entry asks whether an institution, law, social policy, or practice is right, just, good, bad, etc.

7.121 Is a law requiring a person to belong to a union bad?

7.122 Didn't the anti-trust legislation rob people of their rights?

7.123 Do you think the parliamentary system is very good in emergencies?

7.13 The entry asks whether a physical or biological object or characteristic is important, valuable, etc.

7.131 Is the fact that man has the thumb very important?

7.132 Do you think that silicon is very valuable to American industries?

7.14 The entry asks whether an operation is satisfactory, a bit of evidence is sufficient or adequate, or an assumption, statement, conclusion, etc. is true, safe, sufficient, and the like.

7.141 Would that be a satisfactory way to measure humidity?

7.142 Is that a safe argument?

7.143 What about what the newspaper said on toll roads -- is that true?

8. Opining

8.1 Criteria and Examples

8.11 The entry asks for an opinion or belief about the disposition or feeling of an historical individual or social group toward something which happened or existed after his (their) time.

8.111 Would Hamilton favor legislation to help the farmer today?

8.112 Do you think Napoleon would favor present French foreign policies?

8.12 The entry asks for an opinion about how an historical individual or group felt or thought about something which happened or existed during his (their) time.

8.121 How do you think the Romans felt about foreign conquests?

8.13 The entry asks for an opinion about what an individual or group will say or do in the future (immediate or remote) about something.

8.131 What will the next generation say about the administration of President Truman?

8.14 The entry asks for an opinion about whether something is possible or not.

8.141 Can a snake do that -- climb a tree?

8.142 Do you think you can learn to do that -- type 100 words a minute?

8.143 Can one also use 'a = s^2?'

8.15 The entry asks what a person or group lacks, what would benefit him (them), what you (they) would do about something, and the like.

8.151 What do you think the school needs most of all?

8.152 Would an income tax benefit the poor?

8.16 The entry asks for an opinion about whether something is necessary.

8.161 Did President Roosevelt have to declare the bank holiday to save the country from complete disaster?

8.162 Does a fish have to live in water?

9. Classifying

The most (but not completely) dependable verbal cue for the identification of these questions is the occurrence in the question of such words as "group", "type", "class", "classification", "kind", "sort", and other expressions equivalent to these.

9.1 Criteria and Examples

9.11 An instance (either a particular or subclass) is given, and the type (class, kind, etc.) which it belongs to is asked for.

9.111 Is it ("there") usually an adjective?

9.112 What type of reaction is this: exothermic reaction?

9.113 What group (of animals) does the starfish belong to?

9.114 Would this (NaOH) be an organic compound or inorganic?

10. Comparing and Contrasting

The most (though not entirely) dependable verbal earmark of these questions is the presence of such expressions as "difference between (in, among)", "differ", "differ from", "be different", "compare", "like", "correspond".

10.1 Criteria and Examples

10.11 Two or more things are specified, and the differences or similarities between them are to be supplied.

10.111 What is the difference between organic and inorganic (compounds)?

10.112 What do they (words on board) have in common?

10.113 How does that (murder) differ from culpable homicide?

10.114 Is there any difference in the tongue of the lizard and the salamander?

10.12 Two or more objects are mentioned, and their differences or similarities with respect to a specified characteristic or a component part is required.

10.121 Where do we have a big difference in these animals (frogs and salamanders)?

10.122 Can you tell the difference between SO_2 and H_2S as far as the odor is concerned?

10.123 What is the difference in these two (axon and dendron) in their structure?

10.13 An object is specified, and something similar to or different from it is to be supplied.

10.131 What would it (nervous system) correspond to in a building?

10.132 What's the opposite of the word "dorsal"?

10.14 Two or more things are supplied, and the entry asks whether the things are alike, the same etc.

10.141 Is the state the same thing as the government?

10.142 Would a quail be something like a partridge?

11. Conditional Inferring

11.1 Criteria and Examples

11.11 The antecedent gives an objective condition in which a person finds himself, and the question asks what comes to mind, how one would feel, etc.

11.111 What is the one wish that goes through your mind (when you are in a situation that is utterly hopeless)?

11.12 The antecedent mentions or suggests a psychological state (need, want, feeling, use of mind or nervous system, know, perceive, etc.), and the question asks what is to be done, what has to be done, what is going to be done, what you would do, what the result would be, what would be possible, etc.

11.121 If you need a modifier to modify a verb, which one (modifier) are you going to take?

11.122 If you tried to stop thinking, couldn't you?

11.123 If you saw it (cerebrum) from say, the back, what would it appear to be like?

11.13   The antecedent gives a condition, and the question uses such expressions as what happens, what might happen, etc., to ask for the consequent.

       11.131   What happens when you are hypnotized?

11.14   The antecedent gives a condition (action, decision, social practice, etc.), and the question asks for an effect which is good, bad, negative; or the question may simply ask for a value judgment, as in (11.142) below.

       11.141   What are some bad things (which result to the colonies by colonization)?

       11.142   Is he a good judge if he sentences the man to hanging?

11.15   The antecedent gives a condition, and the question uses such expressions as "effect", "affect", "influence", "result", "get", "gain", "give", "bring", to ask for the consequent. Unlike 11.14 above, a descriptive rather than a value consequent is asked for.

       11.151   What else (did the mother country get from having colonies)?

       11.152   Something else (which results to the colonies by colonization)?

11.16   The antecedent gives a condition, and the question uses the expressional form 'What is X...?' to ask for the consequent.

       11.161   If they're (two lines) parallel, what is the altitude of the two triangles?

       11.162   What is the side of the square, if its diagonal is 10?

11.17   The antecedent suggests an operation (mathematical, physical, etc.), and the question asks for the result, outcome, etc.

       11.171   If you put gold in aqua regia, what becomes of the gold?

       11.172   What would result if we were to add this weighter to the beam?

11.18   The antecedent gives a condition (mathematical, physical, etc.) and the question uses such expressions as "how much", "how long", "how many", and other quantitative expressions to ask for the consequent.

       11.181   If you had a car and go fifty miles an hour for three hours, well, how far do you go?

       11.182   If the base is CD, we know its (parallelogram's) here is how long?

11.19   The antecedent gives a condition, and the consequent asks how something may be identified, explained, classified, defined, called, etc.

    11.191   If it (fish's eye) is not compound, what kind is it?

    11.192   When we use this term (friction) in physics, how do we define it?

11.20   The antecedent tells what an object or substance is, and the question asks what it would do, etc.

    11.201   If it's an electrovalent compound, then it would?

12.   Explaining

Entries beginning with How...? and Why...? usually are explanation entries. So, these stems are fairly reliable cues. But if these cues alone are used, many explanation entries will be overlooked. For some of them have quite different stems, such as What...? Is...? Can...? and Would...? The following is a typical case of entries having such stems: 'What else happened that helped business?' The student is asked to cite the event that supposedly "helped business". In general, entries asking for evidence (laws, rules, facts) to account for something are classified under explanation.

12.1   Mechanical Explaining

12.11   Criteria and Examples

    12.111   A physical or biological operation or process performed by, or occurring in, an animal (person) or plant is given, and the entry asks either how or why it occurs or is performed.

        12.1111   How does a chicken digest its food?

        12.1112   Why is it that a frog can live under the water?

    12.112   The entry suggests a physical or biological outcome, result, process, or operation that is prevented or kept, as it is, and the entry asks what it is that prevents it, etc.

        12.1121   What keeps the body temperature from rising on a hot day?

12.2   Causal Explaining

12.21   Criteria and Examples

    12.211   The entry gives a psychological state or attitude (actual or claimed) of a person or group, and asks why it occurs or what brings it about.

12.2111   Why do you suppose the attitude of the President was against the Suez invasion?

12.2112   Why was the main character often unhappy?

12.212   The entry suggests a possible cause of an act (or result), and asks how the suggested cause leads to the given act or outcome.

12.2121   How does socio-economic level lead a person to engage in delinquent activities?

12.213   The entry gives a social or political condition or action, and asks how or why it occurs or has occurred, or what condition causes it.

12.2131   Why did the Democratic party lose the 1952 election?

12.2132   What is the cause of juvenile delinquency?

12.214   A physical effect or outcome (organic or inorganic) is mentioned or described, and the entry asks why it occurs, or what produces it, or what amount of something will produce it.

12.2141   Why does iron rust?

12.2142   Why does a free floating magnet point to the north?

12.215   A state of affairs (organic or inorganic) is described, and the entry asks why or how it is the case.

12.2151   Why is the yellow pine found in the deep south rather than farther north?

12.3   Sequent Explaining

12.31   Criteria and Examples

12.311   This entry states something that happened, and it asks how it happened. Usually the word "happen" occurs in the question and the question usually begins with "How".

12.3111   How did Coolidge happen to become president?

12.3112   How is it that Jackson got the name of Stonewall?

12.312   The entry describes a state of affairs, and asks what some person did that brought it about. These entries usually begin with "What".

12.3121   What had Jackson done that turned the financial interests in the East against him?

12.313   The entry suggests an outcome or result, and asks implicitly what events brought it about. These entries usually begin with "What".

12.3131   What turned the Chamber of Commerce against the NRA?

12.314   The entry states a particular thing that was done by a person(s) other than the one addressed, and asks how it was done.

12.3141   How did he (author of film) show those (ancient fish)?

12.3142   How did Lincoln succeed in winning the nomination?

12.4   Procedural Explaining

12.41   Criteria and Examples

12.411   The entry asks how the person addressed does or did a particular thing.

12.4111   How do you extract it (potassium)?

12.4112   How'd you spell "hydroxide"?

12.412   The entry asks how the person addressed gets or got a particular result.

12.4121   How'd you get the answer to that problem?

12.4122   How do you get that result on those scales?

12.413   The entry asks how the person addressed (or another person or persons) does or did, can (could), or will (would) do a particular thing.

12.4131   How could you prove that the Pilgrims came here for religious freedom?

12.4132   How would you identify an acid?

12.4133   How do they hybridize corn?

12.414   The entry asks how a particular something is done (without regard to time, circumstance, or person).

12.4141   How is sulphur mined?

12.4142   Humidity is measured in what way?

12.4143   "Grandiflora" is spelled in what way?

12.5   Teleological Explaining

    12.51   Criteria and Examples

        12.511   The entry asks why something is important.

            12.5111   Why is the ability to change its
                         color so important to the chameleon?
            12.5112   Can you tell us why rapid communica-
                         tion is important to a nation with
                         a large territory?

        12.512   The entry asks how or why something (exclud-
               ing linguistic and mathematical materials)
               is used.

            12.5121   Why is lead pipe used in plumbing?
            12.5122   How do the various foundations use
                         their money?

        12.513   The entry asks why certain structures
               (biological, physical, or social) exist, or
               why they occur or work in a particular way.

            12.5131   Why are there three branches in
                         our government?
            12.5132   Why do frogs have wrinkled skins?

        12.514   The entry asks why a person or group does
               (did) or would do a particular something.

            12.5141   Why would they (Boxers) pick on
                         that particular city?
            12.5142   Why did he (Arthur Jarvis) leave
                         it (his writing)?

        12.515   The entry asks why a particular situation is
               a problem.

            12.5151   Why are traffic fatalities a
                         problem?

12.6   Normative Explaining

    12.61   Criteria and Examples

        12.611   The entry asks why something is classified
               in a particular way, how it is identified, or
               why it is called what it is called, or it
               asks for a characteristic which is used to
               account for something being or becoming a
               member of a group.

            12.6111   Why do we call them (animals between
                         vertebrates and invertebrates) the
                         chordata animal group?
            12.6112   Why do we put the gypsy moth under
                         insects?
            12.6113   How do we identify spiderwarts?

        12.612   The entry asks how we know something.